WINTER
DIALOGUE

WINTER
DIALOGUE

Poems by Tomas Venclova
Translated by Diana Senechal

Foreword by Joseph Brodsky

Dialogue between Czesław Miłosz and
Tomas Venclova

Northwestern University Press
Evanston, Illinois

Hydra Books
Northwestern University Press
Evanston, Illinois 60208-4210

First paperback edition 1999

Printed in the United States of America

ISBN 0-8101-1726-6

Library of Congress Cataloging-in-Publication Data

Venclova, Tomas, 1937–
    [Poems. English. Selections]
    Winter dialogue : poems / by Tomas Venclova ; translated by Diana
Senechal ; foreword by Joseph Brodsky ; dialogue between Czesław Miłosz
and Tomas Venclova.
      p. cm.
    Poems translated from Lithuanian.
    ISBN 0-8101-1726-6 (pbk. : permanent paper)
    1. Venclova, Tomas, 1937– —Translations into English. I. Senechal Diana.
II. Miłosz, Czesław. III. Title.
PG8722.32.E5A27 1997
891'.9213—dc21   97-2613
                                                     CIP

CONTENTS

Poetry as a Form of Resistance to Reality

Joseph Brodsky

The twentieth century, now nearing its end, seems to have had its way with all the arts except poetry. Viewed less chronologically and more exaltedly, history has imposed its reality on the arts. What we imply when we speak of modern aesthetics is nothing but the noise of history jamming or subjugating the song of art. Every ism is both evidence, direct or indirect, of art's defeat and a scar covering up the shame of this defeat. Though it may be crass to say so, existence has proved capable of defining the artist's consciousness, and proof of this can be found in the means the artist uses. For that matter, any mention of means is, in itself, a sign of adaptation.

The conviction that extreme circumstances require extreme means of expression is now ubiquitous. This idea would have seemed rather odd to the ancient Greeks and the somewhat less ancient Romans, or to the people of the Renaissance or the Enlightenment. Until relatively recent times, means of expression were not grouped in autonomous categories, and there was no hierarchy to them. The Romans read the Greeks, Renaissance readers read both the Greeks and the Romans, and the learned of the Enlightenment read Greek, Roman, and Renaissance authors, without analyzing the way the meter relates to the subject matter—whether it was the Trojan War, bedroom adventures, Adriatic fauna, or religious ecstasy.

As far as literature (and poetry in particular) is concerned, any attempt to use the two world wars, thermonuclear weapons, social upheaval, or the apotheosis of methods of oppression to justify (or explain) the erosion of forms and genres is simply ludicrous, if not outrageous, in its disproportion. The unprejudiced individual cringes at the mountain of bodies that gave birth to the mouse of vers libre.

He cringes even more deeply at the demand during less dramatic times, in periods of population explosion, to make this mouse a sacred cow.

Nothing is more appealing to the sensitive imagination than vicarious tragedy; it provides the artist with a sense of "world crisis" without directly threatening his own anatomy. For instance, schools and movements in painting proliferate precisely at times of relative prosperity and tranquillity. This coincidence, of course, may reflect attempts to recover from, or understand the shock of, disaster. It is more likely, however, that those who have experienced tragedy do not see themselves as protagonists and do not really care about the means by which tragedy is expressed, being themselves their embodiment.

The tragic worldview, the atomization and fragmentation of modern consciousness, and so on are such common currency these days that to articulate them or to use means that allude to them has become little more than a market requirement. The proposition that the market's dictates are essentially those of history itself would therefore not seem merely a heartless exaggeration. The demand for innovation in art, as well as the artist's intuitive striving for novelty, demonstrates not so much the artist's imaginative wealth or the potential of the material as it does art's vulnerability to market realities and to the artist's desire to collaborate with them.

Illogic, deformation, abstraction, discord, incoherence, arbitrary associations, the flood of subconsciousness—all these elements of modern aesthetics, which are theoretically called on, individually or in combination, to express specific qualities of the modern psyche, are in reality strictly market categories, a fact to which the price lists attest. The suggestion that the modern artist's perception of the world is more complex and intricate than that of the audience (not to mention that of his creative forebears) is ultimately undemocratic and unconvincing, for all human activity, both during and after disasters, is based on necessity and subject to interpretation.

Art is a form of resistance to the imperfection of reality as well as an attempt to create an alternative reality, an alternative that one hopes will possess the hallmarks of a conceivable, if not an achievable, perfection. The moment art relinquishes the principle of necessity and comprehensibility, it surrenders its position and dooms itself to fulfilling a purely decorative function. This was the fate of a major part of the European (and Russian) avant-garde, whose laurels still cause many people to suffer insomnia. Both "laurels" and "avant-garde" are, again, essentially market concepts (to say nothing of the strikingly rapid transformation by which the abstract revelations of great avant-garde artists become wallpaper).

The idea of "new means" used by an artist who "outpaces progress" is but a reflection of the romantic notion of the artist as "the chosen one," a demiurge. The proposition that the artist feels, comprehends, and expresses something unattainable by the ordinary person is no more convincing than the suggestion that the artist's physical pain, hunger, and sexual satisfaction are more intense than those of a commoner. True art is always democratic precisely because there is no denominator more common, in either society or history, than the sense that reality is imperfect and that a better alternative should be sought. A hopelessly semantic art, poetry is even more democratic than its relatives, and Tomas Venclova's work is convincing proof of this.

One need only leaf through Tomas Venclova's verse to observe elements that are increasingly scarce in similar publications—first of all, meter and rhyme, the components that shape poetic statement. Because Venclova is a highly formal poet, modern readers brought up on the low-calorie diet of vers libre might identify him with the negative aspects of tradition. Formality and traditionalism, however, are not the same thing. What makes a poet traditional (in the negative, but not the only, sense) is not form but content. And it is enough to read a few lines by Venclova to understand that he is very much a twentieth-century poet. Someone brought up on the above-mentioned diet may ask what makes this poet use formal means that are considered archaic and that, moreover, risk displeasing readers. Is he, perhaps, limiting his scope intentionally instead of widening it through an innovative rejection of formal verse?

To begin with, we should recognize that only content can be innovative and that formal innovation can occur only within the limits of form. Rejection of form is a rejection of innovation. From a purely formal point of view, a poet cannot be an "archaist" or an "innovator" exclusively, for being either is disastrous for content. Tomas Venclova is an "archaist-innovator" precisely in the sense intended by Juri Tynianov in the title of his remarkable book, which contained this phrase until an editor's pen exchanged the hyphen for a fatal "and."

Although Venclova's choice of means is, of course, primarily physiological (if "physiological choice" is not a tautology), it has an extremely serious ethical dimension, one well worth dwelling on. Venclova is the sort of poet who attempts to influence his audience. Poetry is not an act of self-effacement (although it is a possible method); it is an imperative art that imposes its reality on the reader. In theory, a poet eager to demonstrate his ability for self-effacement should not be content with using neutral diction: in theory, he ought to take the next logical step and shut up altogether. The poet who wishes to make his statements a reality for his audience must formulate them as a linguistic inevitability, a matter of the law of the language. Rhyme and meter are his weapons in attaining this goal. It is thanks to these weapons that the reader remembers the poet's language and, in a way, becomes dependent on it; the reader, if you will, is destined to obey the reality created by the poet.

The poet's sense of duty toward language, apart from his sense of social responsibility, determines his choice of means. Language is metaphysical, and often rhyme reveals the interrelatedness of notions and situations in the language that are not registered by the poet's rational consciousness. Sound—the poet's ear—is a form of cognition, of synthesis, that does not parallel analysis but encompasses it. In simple terms, sound is semantic, often more so than grammar; and nothing can articulate the acoustic aspect of a word better than poetic meter. More than a crime against language or a betrayal of the reader, the rejection of meter is an act of self-castration by the author.

The poet has one more duty that explains his devotion to form: his debt to his predecessors, to those who created the poetic language he has inherited. This debt is expressed in the feeling every more or less conscious writer has, that he should write in such a way as to be understood by his ancestors—those from whom he learned poetic speech. Czesław Miłosz feels he should write so that Juliusz Słowacki or Cyprian Norwid would understand him; Venclova believes that his writing should be intelligible to Kristijonas Donelaitis or, say, Osip Mandelstam.

A poet's attitude toward his predecessors is more than a question of genealogy. We do not choose our parents: it is they who choose us by giving us life. They determine the way we look, and they often determine our material circumstances by bequeathing us their fortune—every kind of fortune, including the literal one. Whatever we may think of ourselves, we are they, and they must be able to understand us if we want to understand ourselves. The more they leave to us, the richer is our language, the freer we are in the choice of means, the finer is our ear—our method of cognition—and the more nearly perfect is the world we create by ear.

Form is appealing not because of its inherited nobility but because it is a sign of restraint and a sign of strength. Rejection of form in favor of what are called "organic means" reveals the opposite qualities and implies that the poet's fate and emotions are somehow unusual. But the only thing organic means indicate is the organic nature of melodrama. Apparently, there are two concepts of nature and thus two notions of the natural in art. One goes back, say, to D. H. Lawrence and postulates physiological and linguistic immediacy; the other begins with Osip Mandelstam's line "Priroda-tot zhe Rim, i otrazilas' v nem . . . " (Nature is another Rome and was reflected in it . . .) and has its sequel in the poetics of Tomas Venclova.

Tomas Venclova was born 11 September 1937 in the town of Klaipėda, on the Baltic seashore. His country was living through the last years of its relatively novel independence, and some members of the Venclova family were to play a small but sad part in the loss of that independence. Soon after the partition of Poland, the country in which Tomas Venclova was born became the Lithuanian Soviet Socialist Republic; his father, the poet Antanas Venclova, for a while held a position in the republic's government equivalent to that of minister of culture. Antanas Venclova's leftist convictions played their part in his appointment to this position; it should be noted, however, that the options open to a Lithuanian intellectual in those days were limited: the choice was between communist and fascist sympathies.

The son was to pay rather dearly for the father's choice, particularly at school. A considerable number of Tomas Venclova's classmates saw the boy as the son of a man who had betrayed his country to a foreign power, and they treated Tomas accordingly. The popularity of Antanas Venclova—People's Poet of Lithuania and Stalin Prize winner—did not help, but further complicated the son's position. Such things either scar a person for life, transforming him into a monstrous creature, or temper him. Tomas Venclova was tempered, in large part owing to the aristocratic and artistic influence of his mother's relatives.

At sixteen Tomas Venclova graduated from high school with honors and entered the University of Vilnius, the youngest student in its history. Three years later, however, he was suspended from the university for one year. The year was 1956, when hopes rose with the Hungarian revolution only to die under the treads of Soviet tanks, which literally crushed the rebellion. For Tomas Venclova's generation (and mine), the generation of 1956, the fate of the Hungarian rebellion came to signify what the Decembrists' defeat did for Pushkin's contemporaries or what the fall of the Spanish Republic meant for W. H. Auden and his peers in the 1930s. It not only shaped that generation's worldview but also formed the personal eschatology of many individuals. In any event, our generation was forever lost to the socialist idea.

From another point of view, this generation turned out to be a find for literature; for it started life with less potential for illusions, and the Hungarian tragedy remained its touchstone. At nineteen Tomas Venclova was devouring literature, which became for him the essential reality of existence and, later, his profession as well. He graduated from the university, and for the next twenty years he taught, translated, and wrote journalism and criticism to earn his living; but his life proved to be in writing poetry.

Those two decades saw the continuous growth of his popularity both inside and outside Lithuania. Like his poems, Venclova himself led a largely nomadic life; he constantly traveled about the territory of the last great empire, and his periodic appearances had an obsessive, phantom quality. He stayed for long stretches of time in Moscow and

Leningrad; he met Boris Pasternak and Anna Akhmatova, to whom he became even closer, and translated their works into Lithuanian. He also grew close (sometimes too close) to his contemporaries who wrote in Russian; these relations were to acquire the status of destiny.

Partly because of this mobility, the authorities' constant interest in him never got focused enough to turn disastrous, for the Lithuanian and All-Union KGBs were unable to decide to whose parish Venclova belonged. In the early 1970s, however, after the publication of his first book of poetry in Lithuania, *A Sign of the Language,* storm clouds began to gather quite rapidly over his head. To a great degree the situation was provoked by his active participation in the Lithuanian dissident movement, a commitment that sometimes bordered on foolhardiness. The temporary, though at that time complete, debacle of this movement scattered many of its founders and activists around the labor camps and jails of the empire; some found themselves in emigration. Since 1977 Venclova has lived in the United States.

Tomas Venclova's native languages are Lithuanian, Polish, and Russian. In addition, he has a perfect command of English and Latin, and French, German, Greek, and Italian are not foreign to him either. Possession of three native languages, a result of Lithuania's geography and history, explains the genealogy of the poet and the size of his inheritance. Venclova is the son of three literatures—and a grateful son at that.

Of course, he is primarily a Lithuanian poet, but he is a poet who has absorbed all the best to be found in the neighboring territories. The best of Russia is its language and literature—in particular, its poetry. The same, I am afraid, can be said of Poland. Generally speaking, neither nation—if one looks at its history—deserves its language and its literature. Venclova has not, however, been influenced separately by Polish and Russian poetry; rather, he is a product of their fusion.

Speaking of fusion, though, like speaking of influence, explains nothing of the phenomenon of the poet—or it explains far too little. Nor does biography provide any insights. All these elements create the illusion that we comprehend the phenomenon we call "a poet." The reader may need such an illusion to explain this exception to the existential rule rationally, but the illusion nonetheless has little in common with the reality of the exception. Lithuania has a population of around four million people; a certain percentage of them belong to Tomas Venclova's age group; some of this group have an education in the humanities comparable to his; nevertheless, Venclova's poems could only have been written by him.

We are all infected by the theory of reflection and are convinced that if we know the circumstances of an author's life in detail we will understand his works; we believe that the two are interdependent. In truth, it is independence that links a poem and a life, and it is the independence of the poem from life that allows the poem to be born; were it otherwise, there would be no poetry. The poem and, in the final analysis, the poet are autonomous entities, and no number of retellings, examinations, quotations, or portraits of teachers or of the author can substitute for his work. Venclova's poems are Venclova's life; Venclova's life is the means of their creation, but it has no direct influence on their creation.

Sentiments or circumstances in Venclova's poems may be recognizable, but the manner of their expression is not, if only for the simple reason that the poet's language is Lithuanian. The logic of the images in his work differs from that in Slavic poetry, and even Slavic speakers who can discern his meters could never imagine their sound. We will learn nothing from the fact that Venclova translates into Lithuanian T. S. Eliot, W. H. Auden, Robert Frost, Anna Akhmatova, Osip Mandelstam, Boris Pasternak, Alfred Jarry, James Joyce,

Czesław Miłosz, Zbigniew Herbert, Charles Baudelaire, and William Shakespeare, just as we will not begin to understand him better on learning of his structuralist studies with Juri Lotman in Tartu or by reading the vast bibliography of his literary criticism. Both branches of activity testify as much to the simple everyday necessity of making a living as to his personal tastes. Poems are not dictated by such components of a life; they are dictated by language and by the uniqueness of the human being who writes them—here the man named Tomas Venclova. In a certain sense, it is his poems that are Tomas Venclova, not the heavyset body that, crossing yet another border, shows a United States passport imprinted with this name.

This body has spent fifteen of its fifty-five years outside the walls of its homeland, in "the poor paradise of hard currency"—crudely put, in exile. The poems, however, have not changed place; they continue to exist in Lithuanian. Furthermore, they are destined to live longer than their author. To travel through time, a poem must possess a unique intonation and perception. Venclova's poetry fits this requirement perfectly. His intonation is striking for its restraint and low-key quality, for the conscientious, intentional monotony that seems to be trying to muffle the far too obvious drama of his existence. In Venclova's poems the reader will not find the slightest sign of hysteria or the slightest insistence on the uniqueness of the author's fate, an insistence that logically presumes the reader's compassion. On the contrary, if his poems postulate anything, it is the awareness of despair as a habitual and exhausting existential norm, which is temporarily overcome not so much by an effort of will as by the simple elapse of time.

The attitude of the person evoked by these poems is neither accusatory nor all-forgiving. It could be described as stoic, but not every stoic writes poetry. Nor is this attitude contemplative: the author's body is too involved in the whirlpool of history, while his mind and often his diction are too deeply rooted in the Christian ethic for this label to be apt. The person evoked by these poems might be better compared to a watchful observer, a meteorologist or seismologist recording disasters atmospheric and internal, outside and inside himself. Here it should be added that it is not his eye or his mind that records but his language. Whether that language is called Lithuanian or universal is irrelevant—for Tomas Venclova, the two categories are one and the same.

The lyrical quality of his poetry is fundamental, for as a poet he begins where normal people give up and where the great majority of poets, at best, switch to prose: he begins at the depth of consciousness, at the far limit of joylessness. Venclova's song starts at the point where the voice usually breaks, at the end of exhalation, when all inner forces are used up. In this characteristic lies the exceptional moral value of his poetry, because the ethical focus of the poem is in its lyricism rather than in any narrative element. For the lyrical quality of the poem is in effect a sort of utopia attained by the poet, and it conveys to readers their own psychological potential. In the best circumstances, this "good news" provokes a similar internal motion in readers, moves them toward creation of a world on the level suggested by this news. At the least, it liberates them from dependence on the reality they know, making them aware that this reality is not the only one. That achievement is not small, and it is for this reason that reality holds little love for poets.

Every major poet has an idiosyncratic inner landscape against which his voice sounds in his mind or, if you prefer, subconsciously. For Miłosz, it is the lakes of Lithuania and the ruins of Warsaw; for Pasternak, Moscow backyards with bird-cherry trees; for Auden, the industrial English Midlands; for Mandelstam, a Greco-Roman-

Egyptian collage of porticos and pilasters inspired by the architecture of St. Petersburg. Venclova also has such a landscape. He is a northern poet, born and raised near the Baltic Sea, and his landscape is that of the Baltic in winter, a monochromatic setting dominated by damp and cloudy hues—the light of the skies condensed into darkness. Reading his poems, we find ourselves inside this landscape.

Translated and adapted by Alexander Sumerkin and Jamey Gambrell

WINTER
DIALOGUE

Poems by Tomas Venclova

Translated by Diana Senechal

A Poem about Memory

You wait for those who retreated? To the depths
They have retreated. The walls left them behind,
As did the pictures, pencils, clocks, and souls,
The rain and retribution, sand and snow,
The pine needles, the victory over death.

Already it's unclear which one is right,
And when you calculate the sum of partings,
Your aimless unity explodes inside,
And shatters into voices, fiercely warring.

Nothing is left but a circle drawn by a knife,
Dust on the shelves, a mark upon the plate,
Such stores of freedom, verses and untruth,
And such a shortage of authentic fate.

The warm, unsettling volume of this city
Is touched by the two voices that remain.
To them a drop of memory was given.
You have it. And it is no one's domain.

It runs at random, winged, blind from birth,
Like a swallow that has been cast out from its nest.
And what is all your classicism worth,
That school of ceremony and of jest?

And thus the hour, detaching from us all,
Condemned to death, flutters down just like a shawl
Onto the stairways, corridors, and rooms,

And on the gap, which, disregarding, sprawls
Between the time gone by and time to come.

The twenty-four hours cross the middle, silence grows louder,
Having flown past ears, your words in the dark resound,
And the air smells of wormwood — dry, fake, and bitter,
Since the moon is like coal, and nature is weightless matter.
You awoke long ago. Between yourself and the shores
Of sleep, two planes stretch, merged by a hazy border,
And, at the end of the world, by the farthest height,
The speech of dead leaves, the speech of age-old night.

Will you grasp what the mouth, once silent, whispers aloud?
In the midst of the void, between the black and white clouds,
Above the swampy fields, the light clears the weather
With water reflections, the voice of invisible feathers.
Don't hurry to visit the farm. Like a menace, there lurks
A spring congealed, concealed in the shade of the oaks.
And the owner is absent, and, when the key is inserted,
The days, uninhabited, move in a squeaking circle.

Will you wander further? Beyond the vanishing steam
Of the morning, your time coincides with the ceaseless stream,
And there is no memory able to scoop out the depth,
And childhood is easy, and youth completely bereft
Of meaning. Our souls are nearby, our felling was recent,
The clock of noon is ticking somewhere in the present,
And an arrow halts in the air, having strayed from its line,
Since the world is the same, while solitude changes each time.

Like the hour of death, they await us: the homeward train,
The white postwar dust, the trunk of a half-withered pine,
The fortresses' empty ditches, the beacon in ruins,

And, behind the cracked walls, and open to all, the rooms.
The coolness flows to the coast, the wind takes the leaves,
The light of September grows stronger over the graves,
And, alongside the coast, in the shallow drift, the black
Ships glitter, rich, replete with space and the past.

That's a row of years, of old ages, alien and strange,
Thus, across the hills, the grass becomes one with rain,
Thus the dictionary's thicket splices the objects' fates,
And voices, once lost, return from the world to their place
Inside us. Glance back without fear; I can also feel
How the ponderous breathing burdens our shoulders and heels.
This is just black soil, clay, moisture, oblivion, a well,
The outskirts of others' nonbeing, of others' bells.

You halt amidst driftwood, glass, Cyrillic letters,
In the dead rich streak of the falling tide, together
With companions who left long before their lives had unfolded.
And you, like a shadow, are hidden by heat and enfolded.
And you, disappearing in time, become unaware
Of the onset of fall, of the changes in water and air,
And, larger than its own life, a desolate soul,
Like a scene in the retina, breaks in the depth of the whole.

* * *

A cluster of moraines defines
The hitherto unmelted glacier
Along the railroad track, which winds,
Droning along like a double river
Plunged underground. The banks impend
On high, quelling the resonance,
And suburbs from around the bend
Loom white through chilly voicelessness.

Hiding places, refuge of squalor,
Wire thicket, extinguished garden plot . . .
All of a sudden, springtime's pressure
Engulfs the senses, and, I've thought,
The street seems not to recognize
Itself, now cut off from the park,
The boundary where youth expires,
The space where solitude embarks.

Some wagons can be noticed riding
Through coal and asphalt's land of waste,
While fates no longer coinciding
Criss-cross each other in the past.
The guard of heaven whets the weightless
Light yellow sword, prepared to slaughter
Us both, should we intrude on April,
The realm of snow, the realm of water

Beneath the sun's sphere. Then, at night,
The engines rip into the center;
Having deflected the wick, a draft

Disperses smoke above the concert.
Beside the universe, a chorus,
Beside the sewer, fallen under,
The air shakes sinlessly before us,
As Bach and Mozart would have wanted.

They had conspired to call us into
A strange death. What remains today
Of music, of our common city?
Less than nothing, I would say:
No emptiness, no pitch-black vault,
Which, sealike, would submerge the souls,
But scattered pebbles, poster scraps,
Blotches of paint upon brick walls.

Charon receives the obolus;
Slowly the escalator drifts,
Boatlike, not into Cocytus,
But into Lethe, along the cliff.
The night ignites its final torch.
Having encroached upon our dreaming,
A lifeless ray of light bursts forth
On the other side of time and being.

*   *   *

We'll need them for quite some time yet: to make the path like a deck,
To make your head weigh down, and Syrius breathe more deeply—
The days of the balancing cosmos, heavy as beeswax and nectar,
Filling the yellow jug with sugar, water, and needles.

Not for myself will I see: a shadow, hurled to the earth
From on high, the patches of sun, the coarse warm skin of the pine,
Until the bees strike the glass, resembling phosphorous birds,
Misfortune and poison filling the hives that they left behind.

Glimmer a smile, stand still, then take the path back home—
Outside, the darkness strives to strip the eyes of sight,
But still the syllable, reviving on my tongue,
Will bless and supersede this year's most endless night.
Glimmer a smile, since we are parted by the plain,
The icy lakes, the blizzards, allowing no translucence,
The curtain, which you see as sleep invades your brain,
And murky trains running from Daugavpils to Luga.

The kitchen has a cool spring, drying at the mouth,
And several chairs scattered around like a meager forest.
I also fall asleep, and the meaning of this house
Is just a mailing address, a disk made decaporous.
I also fall asleep; it seems that from the table
I pick up the receiver. It's ruinous to linger,
Since, left with you alone, on waking I am able
To hear myself on the other end when I stop my finger.

*   *   *

I haven't lived here as of old,
And, as I'd walk a voiceless rock
Island, each day I come from far,
And walk this empty river block,
Devoid of stucco, glass, or bolts.

Its rooms are full of sleep and skies,
Its lamps bring darkness to perfection.
Dispersed among the objects' cries,
Between untruth and truth it lies,
An alter ego, a reflection,

A body in a dormant state,
Or news, arriving somewhat late,
Which several seas have washed in passage —
That's why, in substance, form, and weight,
It scares me more, the more I grasp it.

Who, having stayed inside those lines,
Receives the share, with peril rampant,
And keeps the land intact, once granted,
From day's decline to day's decline,
Above the void and present time?

All night, sleep was equivalent to time,
And the city was shooting needles into the face.
I don't know what's in store. Perhaps the currents—
They flash beneath the windows, all the way,
Reflecting the staunchness of the mountain chain.
The snow of the skies, weighing down on the streetlamp,
The arcadia of grasses, the empty squares.
Better to forget. All is untruth, after all,
Only passageways sunken into frost;
Here with your hands you sense the stellar vault,
Porous like stones. Here you would have to live
For centuries—and swim along with the flow
Around each date as if it were an island.
Space filled with dots of light, a heavy crystal
Between the fingers of the Caucasus.
Better to forget. All is untruth, after all.
Experiences, approximations, beginnings.
I can no longer say what touches us:
Perhaps just air, sprouted beneath the snow,
Having taken that night to learn by heart
Our lofty science, rife with imperfections.

*　*　*

The shoots of grass pierce through the face and hands.
Glory to poverty. The earth is made of roses.
The resistance of matter, the soil of Voronezh
Are like the past and like forgotten friends.

Some umpteen planets lie beneath the heart,
And Dante's circles press against the windows,
So close at hand is the path that seeks me out,
Itself now shaken by the ominous ringing.

Joined sentences will scorch the fingertips:
Embittered bread, the weary brain, the fallow
Meadows, whose care is plunged into the valley,
The clan of airy capitals of the sphere. . . .

An Attempt at Describing a Room

o the pillows and the palettes and the earrings made of gold
but the map will never show it as the address is annulled

but the boulevard is glowing and the tea turns into air
but the wires stretch into nowhere and the essence is unclear

tongue of flame begins to flicker midnight strikes you as you write
and the lobsters shrimp and fish break through the canvas with their
    sight

since the border of the fishbowl stretches out our windowpane
where the blind and artless shepherds tend the nutshells in the brine

hardness sets the liquid plaster you i cease to hear or see
void of gratitude and happy underneath the spreading tree

* * *

As in a cloud: a lock, a glass of water, a chair,
And the surface of a door. At three, more or less,
The threshold will be distanced from the tidal star,
So that the floor will never recognize the guest.

Above the bonfire stones, a skyward-spinning thread
Will fade and lose its balance, the grass will feel the burden,
A boat will come untied, and a bird, high overhead,
As always, will outdistance the unfaithful word.

Perhaps the forest warden, deceased, has gone back home,
And wanders in the twilight, not having found a matchstick,
And what nonexistence holds is higher than our own
Existence, and it reaches us like ice and music.

The land beside the stream will crunch beneath the strides,
The unseen hand will touch the heart of the clay earth,
And in your room the bond of objects will arise,
Which, as I understand, has drained space of its worth.

* * *

Like the support of immortal souls,
The world of things behind the windowpane
Flashes, and it's unknown what the future holds
By the imaginary rivers of time.

Will we be able to see their spotted, splashing,
Rust-colored water, washing the houses through,
Once we have traded earthly salt and ashes
For separations, welcoming but few?

Here summer meets its end. A triangular sail
Binds shore to shore like a lock. The blinding sea
Begins to glisten in a glacial manner,
And air, turning to stone, hangs over me.

* * *

We saw each other through another's words,
As through a wall transparent as a pane,
While, for the one who had invited us,
No longer than a month of life remained.

Just like the ticking hand, the spirit turns,
Weary of the unearthly tonal spectrum;
Inside us, generations take new forms,
As, long ago, Mnemosyne directed.

Winter withdraws into its nest to show
It couldn't save us, after all. Between
The cities, between the nadir and the zenith,
Just like a garden, silence murmurs low.

Above the promontory, the day emits its last.
How dazzling the heat, how harsh the vault in splendor.
The foam construction, which the coastline tore asunder,
Comes back to life like a flame flickering in the grass,

Or like the plains of sand, or like the depth of bays . . .
Their speech in its opacity makes ours seem light and shallow.
No sound in memory. As from a fortress cellar,
From inside the consciousness the wellspring breaks its way.

So nature overcomes us. The resonating sand
Comes gushing through the doors. The lighthouse starts to speak
As would an angel of judgment. Salt eats away the lock,
And clouds obscure the sun and weigh upon the land.

* * *

To the squares on our walls and floors,
And squares upon the doors,
To the high windowpanes—twice more,
And to the lamp—twice more,
To names of amputated shores,
To gates of maps, and to
The air not being jumbled, or
The inside jumbled too.
To locomotive wheels that roar,
Keys tested long before,
To all of us, those two times four,
Those times that number four.
To that which from the wires will pour,
Which ice cannot ignore,
To two and two still making four,
And two times two—still four.

Enter this landscape. Darkness still prevails.
Filled to the brim with voices, though unseen,
The continent takes arms against the seas.
Across the dunes, the empty highway wails.
A passerby or an angel in the snow
Has left a subtle covered trail behind,
And, in the blackish pane, the seaside's glow
Becomes the bleak Antarctic in our minds.

The chasm, not frozen, froths beneath the land.
The pouring grains of sand pass their first mile.
Sometimes the pier grows vivid, sometimes veiled,
And, menacing, the winter space expands.
No telegrams, no letters stay behind,
Just photographs. No sound from the transistor.
A candle, you would say, had sealed the time
Of danger with its burning hot wax drippings.

How sonorous the rock, how damp the air,
How mighty the roentgen when it forestalls
The dawn! You strain your eyes until the walls,
Church tower, human body turn transparent.
Only the hazy contours of the trees
Stand out against the whiteness. Through the bark,
Even closing your eyes, you almost see
The stubborn, narrow last ring of the trunk.

"This habit has been trying on my eyes;
In just a minute, I will surely falter."
"The prophesy is speaking of another."

The hoarfrost-covered axis now inclines,
And, at the line of the horizon, where
The ships turn black, where the vibration freezes,
A flame bursts forth from Mars and Jupiter,
Deep in the sluggish sky, above the seaside.

The void extends to the Atlantic sand.
The field gapes like a hall, open and barren.
While January blankets February,
The plain shrinks back from the watery wind.
Past the lagoons, the hills begin to bare
Themselves; the somewhat melted snowdrift stiffens
And darkens in the pit. "And what is there?"
"Again the ports and bays, the mouths of rivers."

Beneath the meshes of the weighty cloud,
The squares, like fish, are glittering and playing.
"Do you remember what the stars were saying?"
"This century is managing without
A sign; there's just statistics." "Gravity
Of death has fettered person, plant, and thing,
But sprouts burst forth from seed and sacrifice,
And then not all is over, or so I think."

"Where is the witness? Still it's not too clear
What separates the real from the imagined;
Perhaps just you and I are on this planet."
"It seems to me that only you are here."
"And what about the third one? Do you mean
That no one hears us talking, or takes part?"

"There is the firmament and snowy green,
And the voice, at times, lives longer than the heart."

The stroke of noon brings dark hues to the woods.
When day attains its height, the consciousness
Retains light things, brought forth from nothingness
A moment ago, taking the place of words:
A piece of ice, split into particles,
A skeleton of boughs, a brick wall, crumbled
Beside the roadway's bend . . . Then all is silence
On this side of the sea, and on the other.

*   *   *

I was welcomed by twilight and cold.
Past the stark and ponderous arches
Some ten stations began to unfold,
And umpteen November parks:
This circle, or settled place,
Where the beam of a hundred-watt bulb,
Conducting into the maze,
Deceptively hits the brick wall.

The realm of Ariadne and Minos
Can become a new home, though soon ended;
Because of the fog, not one plane
In the past few hours has ascended.
How packed are the trains, every day —
So much space, so much air and hardship!
Thus the prisoners, wending their way
Homeward, sometimes ached for the guard.

Like a debt that space was repaying,
The places I knew came uncovered.
"University, bus," I was saying,
"Island, monument," over and over.
I said: "Tomorrow I'm leaving,
Or at least I will try to depart."
And there, at the edge of the living,
My soul plunged into the dark.

Old street names and numbers came closer,
Form and meaning had changed in each letter.
I followed the vanishing voices,

Unable to find us together
In the apartment, bolted and empty,
Where the pictures don't know me, nor even
In dreams, or the kingdom of heaven,
Or the second circle of Dante.

Thus time is cut short: to be clear,
One does not break the habit of living,
Only, I would say, with each year,
From farther you hear the phone ringing.
Only memory, as the days pass,
Widens itself like a compass,
Until a straight line is the past
That once made a pretense at distance.

In reality cut from reality,
What you hear or perceive, I don't know.
The paved banks of the Acheron
Withstood the insensible flow.
Each nothingness stands on its own,
And without us the world still persists,
And the Muses and silence alone
Can, in truth, be said to exist.

Where the capital spins in a ring,
And the snow games make us weary,
Where the fog won't betray the things,
Thank God for the dictionary.
In the land where the hand of a friend
Never rushes to help one in anguish,

The highest power, or the void
Sends the angel down: rhythm and language.

I don't ask for a minute's oblivion,
Or death, or sins' forgiveness,
But leave the primordial moan
Over icy night and stone.

In Petersburg we will come together anew.

Osip Mandelstam

Did you return to the once promised place,
The city's skeleton, reflection, trace?
A blizzard swept the Admiralty away,
The geometric hue fades into gloom
Upon the surface.
                     Turning off the electric
Current, a shadow rises from the spectrum
Of ice, and rusty steam engines, like specters,
Near Izmailov Prospect rise and loom.

The same tram, the very same threadbare coat . . .
The asphalt makes a shred of paper float
Above it, and the nineteenth-century cold
Submerges train and station.
                        Wailing skies
Enclose themselves. The decades turn to mist,
The murky cities pass, like storms adrift,
The gestures are repeated, like a gift,
But from the dead a man does not arise.

He retreats into a February morning,
Which has encompassed Rome, sluggish and northern,
Into another space, choosing a rhythm
Approximated to the hour of snow.
He's summoned to the she-wolf's lair, now frozen,
The mental institution, filth and prison,

The black, familiar Petersburg, arisen
In someone or other's speech some time ago.

Not harmony, nor measure, once they're quelled,
Return to life, nor the crackling, nor the smell
Inside the hearth, which time has kindled well;
Yet there exists a timeless hearthlike focus
And optics, mapping destiny, whose essence
Consists of fortunate coincidences,
Or simply meetings and continuations
Of what is neither temporal nor local.

No image, but a breach in what is known,
An island, grown into the current's foam,
The substitute for paradise unshown
Arise in living language. In the shower
Of clouds, above the stem of a ship afloat,
The pigeons move in a giant circle, not
Presuming to distinguish Ararat
From any ordinary hill in flower.

Forsake this shore. It's time. We will embark.
The lie runs dry, the stones are split apart,
But there remains a single witness: art,
Bringing light into the nights of winter's depth.
The blessed grasses overcome the ice,
The mouths of rivers find the bays at night,
And a word, as meaningless as it is light,
Resounds, almost as meaningless as death.

* * *

Desist, desist. The crumbling sentence dies.
The rooftops' limit verges on the dawn.
The snow speaks forth, the fire in fugue replies.

The swinging of the pendulum subsides;
The leaden counterbalance marks the ground.
Desist, desist. The crumbling sentence dies.

Reflected in the mirror's wasteland eyes,
Instead of the world, an outline gleams alone.
The snow speaks forth, the fire in fugue replies.

And back into the cell the captive strides,
And skyward wades the fencing of the zone.
Desist, desist. The crumbling sentence dies.

A grain of time, a splinter of the skies
Envelops both our bodies, like a globe.
The snow speaks forth, the fire in fugue replies.

Things cling to the face only to vaporize,
And heads of beds have no angels around.
Desist, desist. The crumbling sentence dies.
The snow speaks forth, the fire in fugue replies.

* * *

We've been seized by the pull of the universe since September began.
Shut your eyes, and you'll sense how a leaf, having brushed past the
    face,
Flutters into the shutter, and brushes a cloud by mistake,
And gets stuck in the tile, so as not to be reached by the hand.

The tree drains the day. The heavens are blinded and white.
Wading into the waterfall valley, the voice is receding.
I have been singled out to grasp how the stillness inside
And the steam of the bath brought gladness to wearied Atrides.

Will you conquer this threshold? Destiny, castle, crushed stone,
Wretched churches of flint, muddy triangular spaces,
Into putrid decay, into sand the expansive hour pours,
The metropolis soars, and the twelve winds swoop upward to chase it.

Will you win me or lose—in the meantime there's no way to learn.
These soils have gone shallow, the constellar thicket is felled.
I'm attracting misfortune, just as the north pulls a magnet,
As magnet pulls magnet, misfortune attracts me in turn.

To the memory of Konstantin Bogatyrev

Midcentury has overtaken me.
I lived, but learned to nonexist at that.
Death came along and joined the family,
Claiming the greater portion of my flat.
I'd try to make her tame, little by little,
Imploring her not to extend her hand,
And, in the mornings, I'd observe the city,
The loveliest on Eastern Europe's land,
As far as I know: where iron awaits its stroke,
Where rotting rushes rustle in the mist,
There's a locomotive, knuckle-duster, rock,
And, possibly, some gasoline at best.
Within this death, I'd sleep, I'd drink, I'd eat,
I'd try to give her a meaning and a goal,
I'd even let her slip my mind. But meet
Her casually—that's almost impossible.

I'd turn the key in the corridor. The breath
Would lose its rhythm; the heart would drop its weight
Onto the chest. To tell the truth, death
Could even be fortuitous in this state.

THE SHIELD OF ACHILLES

To Joseph Brodsky

I speak, if but to see upon the screen
Of nerves, as you once saw, in vivid tones,
The fences near the chapels of stone,
The key beside the ashtray dumped clean.
You were not wrong: it's all the same as here.
Even the volume of imagination.
The same kilometers toward the ocean,
        Which lends an ear

To us at night. Under the roof of leaves,
The heavy lamps are almost alike in shining.
The different tempos in the chimings
Suggest more danger than the bitter wave
Dividing us. Withdrawing into space,
You turn into an unknown, like the Medes
And Greeks. We remained on this ship to meet
        Only disgrace—

Since it's not safe, not even for a rat.
Examine it: it's not a ship at all,
But shining roofs, calamities, brick walls,
The date recurring all too fast—
In a word, the age of maturity. Its wardship
Seeps through to the marrow, and its space,
Growing more waste each day, would blur the gaze,
        If, by the border

(The ruminating ground for upright rain),
The solemn arch of sound were not to arise,
Almost destroyed in this summer of surprise,
But instead presenting us with blessed chains
Which coincide, probably, with the soul—
They stigmatize, determine, raise the form,
Because our skies, because our *terraferma*
        Are the voice alone.

Peace be with you. Peace be with me and you.
Let there be darkness. Let the seconds tumble.
Through dense vastness, through layers of slumber,
I split your words apart and read them through.
The cities disappear. In nature's stead
There's just a white shield, which has outweighed
Nonbeing. Both our eras will be played
        Out on its face

(If only force and time were not so stingy!)
As in the water. Or, to be exact,
As in the emptiness. The billows thrash,
Wiping away the living scene. The windows
Glisten in squares of blackness. In a dream,
The heated air sifts through the glass slowly.
Far in the distance, past the towers, screams
        A motor, rolling

The hours onto me. At times one can see
In the dark: you see a bell swaying,
You see an endless interval fraying,

While the foundation answers silently.
The stricken portals shudder, growing tight,
The arch sends out a signal to its neighbor,
And souls and continents invoke each other
        In the breathing night.

The dirty fog sticks to the sails at dock.
The wet embankment warms and clouds with steam.
You see Thermopylae, and Troy you've seen—
You have received a shield. You are a rock.
Pillars, erected on that fortitude,
Plunge sparkling metal into the wind,
Although not far from stillness does it stand,
        Or from untruth.

Entrusting us with all our destinies,
You enter the plateau of recollections.
But every moment, doubled into fractions,
And twinning light becomes our company
Inside a circle, narrowing more and more.
Low tide. The sand is patched with gleaming puddles.
The eye still can't distinguish stone from rudder
        On the empty shore.

How is this, Elpenor, how could you journey to the western gloom
swifter afoot than I in the black lugger?

Odyssey 11.57–58

I suppose this never happened. Through the branches
We saw a large and desolated harbor.
The concrete pier was bleaching peacefully
In shade, on the water encumbered with silt.
The splintered piles protruded from the breakers.
The wind, once barely leaping above the plain,
Now teased the sandy whirlpool, darker than
The smashed ribs of the vessels. The savage air,
Transfixed by masts, entwined in ropes, lay heavy
Upon the thistle, the dunes, the stretch of water.
On the horizon, the heat was fluttering,
As a tattered flag might. A fellow who
Had hammered up a raft of rotten planks
Took it for a ride through the stream. It seemed
He would have been heartened by some companions.
Besides him, we saw no one on the shore.
Someone had told us once that this site,
Like many sites, resembled Ithaca.

We stood there, in the focus of the day.
The war of bygone ages and the voyage
Were filling our brains, just as a wave
Fills up the bronchus of a reckless swimmer.
Crunching beneath our feet: the mussels, bones,
And porous pebbles. Then we lay down on
The grass, with nature off our minds. And nature
Had cleared us from her mind long before.

The firmament flowed by. The rumbling salt,
Incited by the shrouded moon, rehashed
Its cycle. Floats were soaking in the sea.
Upon the logs, bound together by iron,
Beneath the sun's full blaze, the mollusks glittered.

What murkiness, what patient depth arrives
With every breaker! How the foam resounds—
Now in memory's hole, now close at hand,
Between the dredger's backbone and the pier.

An evanescent rustle passed us by:
A traveler, bearing an oar on his shoulder,
Headed for the land, where no one ever
Had seen an oar. And, at the foot of the dune,
A field mouse, darting, shot a sudden eye
At the trident rusting on the sand.

There is no wave. Rather, there is a force,
But not the sum of drops. Within each second,
The water parts with itself. Equator of death,
Cramped island, grass beneath the palm of the hand,
Return, change. Not even this
Is promised us by history and myth.

Beyond the bend, a change crept over the scene.
At first the perspectives moved slightly.
Each grain of sand, gleaming along the way,
Came to our eyes through a magnifying glass,
And rocks appeared through reversed binoculars.
The outlines of the objects blurred, as would

Sounds in a shapeless hall. Soon all of us
Concluded that the heat must be the cause,
And suffered no surprise, when, by the warehouse,
We met a friend—the very first of those
To be encountered only after death.

He was the first.

SESTINA

It's roughly six o'clock, and the ice-covered road
Swerves to the north. Tied to the tires, the chains
Rattle the road. A voiceless steel echo,
Like the lake's surface, glimmers a reflection.
The weightless wound-encumbered March snow
Still tries to cover the demolished forest.

Like a raft, splitting apart the static forest,
The glance halts. It is deluded by the road,
The severalfold self-duplicating snow,
And birches making monotonic chains.
In the mist, the well-sweep rises reflecting
The empty house. And all the rest is echo

And clots of air. An aimless, homeless echo,
Which does not exist, sends rumbles through the forest.
The graphite mirror blackens, reflecting
The vaulting dark. We have been given a road
And sky-born, sky-matured, sky-banished chains:
Invisible, but all-consuming snow.

Spring's old age falls beneath the watch of snow,
And the hearing is ripped by the many-faced echo.
Like a dam, wresting its way out of its chains,
A blind thought soaks itself into the forest.
Here gasoline won't help, not the white road,
Nor the clearing strip, unfolding its reflection.

The formless universe pours its reflection.
A shiver-giving star, the reason-stealing snow

Besiege the plain and arm themselves for the road.
Reflection, shadow, reproduction, echo
Refill the overtumbled Arden forest;
Their changes constitute the only chains.

Will we be ever tempered by Thy chains?
All things and elements rise, reflecting
Myself. I will forsake this murky forest,
Where trees are cloaked and guarded by the snow,
And words give over to a futile echo,
And all comes to an end. Perhaps the road

Itself is chains. I am denied the road
Into Thy forest. The earth is numbed by snow.
We're enemies reflecting. Thou art an echo.

Outside the doorway ends the land.
From far a wave rolls to the sand.
The light appears to break the band
That binds the wind and stone.
Time had no name when I was born,
But rifts had broken up the shore
(The gravel glitters even lower,
Where hints of dawn are sown).

The rugged rays, unsparing, tear
And crack the asphalt here and there,
The needles guzzle midnight air
Upon the roofs of slate.
The coal will make the future bright,
The future will dissolve at sight,
And then a child will fear the night,
And sleep into escape.

No oxen standing at the door,
No fame, no Magi are in store,
But there will be enough space for
The Lord, if, past the pane,
A solitary creaking pine,
Vault, axis of the world, inclines,
And the cradle will be called divine,
As will the hearth and flame.

Upon the line where eyes meet air,
Together with the babe, I fare
Along the slope of breathing, bare

And fearful to the sight;
I listen, hurry, memorize,
I speak, and don't know who replies:
The One transcending all divides
Or else a ring of light.

As in a photograph, unsafe and vast.
The skies retreat from roofs, as sea from masts,
Having absorbed the city's white disease.
An early frost transfixes every word,
Singeing the mouth and lungs until they burn,
Inside the empire by the locked-up seas.

Not even a small sign comes from the past,
The black sun beats and grinds into the floor,
And one day voyages will meet their end,
Where birthplace, deadlock, burden all extend,
Severe, without a chance of death or cure,
And Paestum columns sink in the morass.

Tuesday. Clear weather. Winter is at hand.
The Finnish skerries lie, gripped by the low land
That binds the harbor like the heart of sleep.
And maybe then, or maybe once already,
The hour disintegrates above the eddy,
And time reincarnates into a sweep.

Although I won't be able
To lose you, yet I will,
I'll put out every taper:
The tower and the bell,
The stony streets, the shore
Bespecked with tar, and even
My soul, though I'm not sure
It counts among the living.

Here, underneath my feet,
The shaky roadway crumbles.
The shooting range, unlit,
Conceals a dark-voiced rumble
Of waves, a vast expanse,
And, from the days of Noah,
Above the depths, the dance
Of Aquilon and Notus.

Fires of loneliness sail
Above the salt abyss,
Above death's crystal hall.
There empty trolleys stream
Around the theater's corner,
The crowds of bridges swim,
And a lifeless pine-filled forest
Moves stepwise in a dream.

I cannot see Orion,
But the spume of billows glows.
The clouds, in double row,

Let the horizon through.
The wet tree seems a nerve
Beside the wretched granite,
And Aquilon and Eurus
Revolve the sky around it.

Will you disappear or wallow
In my eyelids' darker side?
Having closed my eyes, I follow
The final splash of light.
Eternity will flood us,
But under my hand these stall:
The patience of your garden,
The weight of your stone walls.

No fortresses, no laurels
Adorn the trampled wild,
The grass that poked the holes in
The tense magnetic field,
The void, dripping, decaying,
Soaking the head in chill,
And frenzied Boreas flaying
Beyond the nameless hill.

The clear gust of the ether
Finds echoes in the grasses.
Will you rule or will you wither
In memory's recesses?
It seems that ruin prevails —
And, guilty to the brim,

My greedy mouth assails
Your remnant oxygen.

Time inundates the road.
The cliffs approach in haste.
May Aeolus, if God
Is absent, keep you safe.

Two Poems about Love

I

When, in private, tottering wisdom is sent from a height,
And fragments of stairway chatter come rolling down,
Above the muddy garden, befriended by night,
Above the wasteland, flutes and harps are born.

Beneath the sandy slope, the dry riverbed
Comes to life, the round drop pierces the steaming stone,
The orchestra's rumble rises, the end is ahead,
Which, as you know, requires neither word nor form.

Salt on the mouth. The brine bespeckles the brow.
The city sprawls like a whale cast onto the sand.
A twisted fragment of space, by which the reckless
White flight of converging souls will come to an end.

An angular star gleams in the slit of the eyes,
The impulsive universe provides a galactic lens,
And your life — a swallow surmounting the earth — alights,
And burdens the shoulder, and flutters, and makes no demands.

It's not worth looking around; we are long surrounded,
Confined in the muddle of aerial waterfalls,
Invisible landslides, gray clouds, melody bounding —
It fills the mouths and sticks to the alveoli.

And all returns. I remember those verses by heart.
Having tilted, the sleepless houses turn to the left.

Under ridges of roofs, the darkness is spread apart,
And the wearied hands turn the sky like a sail adrift.

II

The streets lose their names, I await no more guests,
The iamb of others is absent at best,
And even, it seems, the heavens, forbidden,
Have abandoned my thoughts. But space has remained,
For the glittering water floods in, all the same,
And carries the overturned tower along with it.

Three dimensions squeak, like the linkage of mail.
The reflection plays with them; when the skies pale,
It fades, and the empty abode receives
Maybe darkness of May, maybe darkness of June,
And a lifetime is short, and that is untrue,
Since the lamp, in the meantime, protects us from evil.

Don't rush, it's not time. The children still sleep,
The miracle waits to be born. Pools and creeks
Grow cold, roofs blacken, and summertime ripens,
And voices and landscapes in separate dreams
Pass each other like boats. When day sends its gleam,
We'll endeavor to misunderstand them, most likely.

The sonorous-dark, cloven thicket of forms
Oppresses our consciousness; it's not known
Whether even one line coincides, or a fraction,

But the bodies, like stones, still lie side by side,
And the fortress grows clear in the quadrate of light,
And Cassandra's epiphanies lose their attraction.

* * *

Write a poem about a conversation with birds.

From a letter

Although the well is bottomless and steep,
The oriole, reed, human, constellation
Dare to peer into the brilliant deep—
United by an unforseen relation.

It often seems that this is all the same
One light refracted through a sounding prism.
Your truth and dust, what difference can they claim
From all the thrush's silvery sophisms?

Before the dawn, when summer ends its course,
When the vault scatter and worlds fall to the ground,
One and the same unconscious, sightless force
Strikes you, a frail lyre, into sudden sound.

✳ ✳ ✳

At a glance the room is brought to clarity
Anew, losing its ballast in a rush:
The mixture of a few realities,
Which circumscribes the thorax after dusk.
The book and placemats return to their place,
As does the rumbling jet, the September rains.
In the hewed-out gap in the universe (perhaps
Behind the pane) the lindens have been detained.

Like us, they have succumbed to failure's blow.
Like rigging, disengaging from a sail,
They try to break asunder, but night's flow
Makes place and time their unremitting jail.
Be one with their translucence and their dark.
Glance through the glass. Like an atom in the sky,
Its circles tangent to the branches' bark,
An aerodrome is glittering nearby.

A jet descends into its nest. Submerged
Deep under it, the disc glitters and narrows.
On the surface, the paths of space converge.
Denouement. Things hit a point like arrows:
Prophetic visions; separations; death,
Which chose us (and perhaps brought us to be);
The whiteness of a page. And memory, left
Above us like a star above the sea.

Inside the wasteland, in the heart of sleep,
When you have stopped, your palms hiding your face,
For the umpteenth time befriend yourself, and speak,

Hearing a muffled echo out in space,
Filling the vault (just as a tempest fills
A shell): "I have no wish to be a judge,
But helpless, I can't help. Here there is
No verdict, no reward, no remedy."

* * *

In the indigent cities, it's time to leave friends behind us.
The floating lamps shed their barren light in blessing.
The night loses us; the bumpy pine forests, resin
And needly sky of the road to Aukštadvaris find us.

Yes, this is Thy space that suddenly grows and thickens.
Thou drawest us near, then far from the finish line.
Thou contractest my pupil, after stretching the field of vision
To the shadow of the hand, to the tarpaulin, moist and blind.

And if my generation is not destined to win the race,
May the first one not feel the need, in his short life to follow,
Of his daily bread and not-so-everyday fate,
Of his daily salt and not-so-everyday water.

May they find me at last: his perfect voice, broken away,
The atonement for untruth, the beginning of trouble and freedom—
Thus the Nemunas water is bound to be black and sweetish,
That the waning moon, turning to vapor, may float to the bay.

GHETTO

We'll certainly return here. This is peace.
So many homes. With the uncanny ease
Of coal, all has been numbered, weighed, divided.
This is the final hour.
                        Betrayal tightens
And seals the glass displaying random bits
Of news, flows through the doorway's yellow chink,
Colors the armband, condemns the bond and ink
To death, and loads a burden on the nets.

Ah, childlike thoughts, a house on shaky grounds,
Abated waters, artificial mounds!

There is no death, and judgment will not come.
The window's frame is licked by sand and flame.
No more by laws of ancient Hebrew times,
Or Roman—by the one and final law
We are no more than letters, footnotes, dashes.
We are untainted paper. We are ashes.

REPETITION WITH CHANGES

When, in the midst of August, past
a hundred lakes, a hundred rivers,
in self-abandonment, you gasp
that aimless name, when the syllable

ebbs from the lips, and when you sense
that the lips are dry, the streets lack air,
when, in the heat of night, whose tense
grip holds your voice, you disappear,

since nights are the support of sound,
beside the church, the bolted station,
the store that reaches to the bounds
of a universe bound for extinction,

beneath the ground or beneath the clouds
(since chasms are replaced by skies,
and, from the ash foliage, a bird,
the essence of the dark, arises),

and when a shout (or perhaps a song),
usurping oblivion, hovers,
the very nature of matter is long
distance, removal from one another.

In voices there cannot exist
present or past. Where you will be,
or I (also within night's midst,
in the second half of this century,

in the middle of August), it's all the same
what will poison us, what will rise
in our defense, since, likewise aimed
at its source, a word deprived of rights

will reach us, or a word's remains,
a mortal reflection of light, flitting
in the beyond, where, like two swords,
two darknesses, two lives are meeting,

a match inside a well-locked house,
succumbing to the midnight's beckon,
will seize the blindness, drawing forth
if just the contours. If just a second.

A Poem about Friends

For Natalia Gorbanevskaia

When even strangers lose the marks of strangeness,
And all those things that had no chance to pass
Leave downward with the flow of nonexistence—
Assuming nonexistence has a path—
When, past the city, day comes to a close,
And, following a storm, the radio rumbles,
We won't be able to turn or lock ourselves
Outside of the last minutes of this summer.

The air grows dark; through the doors enter
The exiled, the detained, the disappeared,
For whom, this very night, out room turns into
The only possible Elysian field,
The ones whose shadows wander in our dreams,
Those who have loved each other and forgotten,
Make the depths of mirrors their uncertain home,
And, without warning, rise up from the bottom.

Thus they are raised from the dead underground:
The winged women and the unseen brothers,
The generation long reduced to sound,
To margins, or to grass thirsting for water,
And those who live are chosen by the fog,
Deserted houses, journeys into the distance,
Their weapons are staunchness, abstinence from speech,
And possibly, Apollo's own assistance.

The rooftop will resemble Nature's verge,
The night will disentangle thaw from frost,

And, even with death nearby, the spoken word
Will nonetheless be worthy of our trust,
If, poisoning all thought and all sensation,
And hollowing a hole in stone stairs,
An uninvited future should await them:
The object they gave up and then made theirs.

They frequented our forests. Like the pines,
Dead furniture preserves the finger smudges.
Now, having met the maturity of time,
They no longer depend on earthly judges.
It is an open, ample family,
Whose children have been given just one name—
And emptiness, forcing the voices free,
Refills our vacuum up to the very brim.

I do not believe in calamity, but rather
In friends, to whom I dealt in equal shares
The distance separating eyes from matter:
Infinity, unnatural and scarce.
All faces disappear into the light,
The lamps flicker out, truths become divulged,
But footsteps reach a meeting point inside
Myself, just as parallel lines converge.

And again it's autumn, full of lavish folly.
Inside the city, which some souls have won,
Above the alien trolleycars and dwellings,
At this very hour, September has begun.
Imposing barges stand affixed to piers,

Since morning, every nerve is wound up tight,
And, on the road, the first leaf that appears
Is crooked, like the armor of a knight.

At the foot of the slope, the marsh stinks of metal.
A horse nibbles the echinodermal blades.
Eight women toil at tables at the center
Of autumn and the plain. Dew saturates
The Ohio weekend. Down in the ravine,
A maple tree is rusting (or a can,
No way to tell). Lights thickening their beams,
Wisconsin, the Dakotas, Oregon,

Orion too. The landslide of the Lord
Onto the lost space. While the monotone
Of heartbeats smashes the severe ground,
Let thanks be given for the new land.
I can't see through it, but it is alive.
It can't see through me, yet I would assume
That the aged dog would sooner recognize
Odysseus here than in his native home.

I offer my thanksgiving for the answers,
Which the sleepless mind is weary of pursuing.
For the new water. For grasses belonging
To the future. For the patient wind
Over them. For the grave in the foreign land,
For the weight of the foreign stone, not killing,
For nonexistence. And for Thee, Who can
Draw something from it. If Thou dost will it.

For the black music of the spheres. And for
The containment of it in this day's rotation.
Accustomed to the twilight, the objects are

Repeated on this side of the ocean.
The corners fill, as three clocks arise.
The retina, not fearful of mistakes,
Discovers a lock, a tablecloth, the stars
Just as in childhood, in the same old place.

From the mouth of a dragon
the Baltic waters come pouring. A bronze claw flashes,
the sharp-edged current, curling up whiplike, lashes
itself into steam
at the fountain's mouth.
No instant cure can be found for memory's breaches,
and, above Copenhagen, the familiar rain cloud approaches
from the left,

if you look to the south.
They are joined by tin roofs, by branchless mud-covered lindens,
by bicycles, thousands of bicycles. Hastily hidden
in the water, an echo has leaped
to the surface, beside the port's gates.
The asters are damp. The attics parade their geraniums loudly,
the vertical line of the barge entraps the sidewalk, resounding
in the channel, whose depths

are opaque. You might say
only statues can conquer this autumn. The wet king extends
his hand to the bishop. The letters, the crosses engraved on the stands
are nibbled away
by the void of brine,
since history ends. The countries and states disappear.
Having lent your ear, you can hear: from the pole October draws near,
and winter behind.

The dim neon pounds
on the boulevard corner. A traveler sets down his bags,
looks at Anna's square, touches the branches, silently asks

what city he's found,
since the day
overflows with the black taste of home. A sailboat bumps
the shore, and the name from the north, the crowded consonant lump
in the mouth, rolls smoothly away.

The solid stucco is laden
with crucified bindweeds, with leaf-stars and roses,
a resonant railroad past Tivoli opens and closes,
the incoming train
is never delayed.
Not that thing called beauty lies under the pupils, but sand
mixed with lime, a cheek's contour, the touch of a hand,
the horizon's line.

You're compelled
to let your shoulders fall back on the strengthening wind,
to scoop up the salt and silt you know, but within
the inscrutable well
the level falls every second,
and so many times you have offered thanksgiving and paid
for your exile in cash, having chosen your personal fate.
You won't answer the beckon

of home, since each atom stationed
in your body has long been replaced. Dislodged, the
consciousness fumbles
through language, as if through a drawer. Moods, adjectives humming,
negations,
the blindness

of infinite particles, crowded sentences, and, only now and then,
the dry, as if unfamiliar, but breath-stopping pain
and silence.

A cloudburst of rays
sets a crown on the spiral tower. You pass a brick wall
as if you blew out a candle. Baroque architecture must fall
as dictated by space,
and, instead of the bricks,
beyond the bushes and wasteland, sand meets the debris
of *mare*, *pelagos*, *thalassa*, sea, the singular sea,
as wide as the Styx.

And over the brinks
of the crests, and over the breaches of foam,
the lead converges in piles, predicting oblivion and storm.
The flat mainland stinks
of squalid ore,
and the radio misfires. There remains of the homeland, all told,
just a soundless threat, a leaking uranium whale
on the crags of the shore.

For now, you exist.
The granite directs the stage; with the willows' cues
in the face of noon, the park sheds its yellow leaves,
the barometer clenches its fist
at the shimmering depth.
The cold pierces through to the bones. No salvation from sweater
or jacket,

and Telemark ice is the wind, and fog is the breath of Kattegat,
and death is death.

All told, this prevails: apprehending the sound of a punctual train,
caressing the face of a stranger, hands on the rails,
when, in error, the whole dictionary
coincides with the pronoun "we."
The magnesium frost gives a glow to the tray, the sheets,
and the traveler clenches his teeth, numbly shooting the seed
to the depths of the wearied womb.

Never again
to go home. To wrap yourself up, and vanish
in the fortress of fall, relinquish what you must relinquish,
and this still ahead,
a trace of the previous land.
And hearts are still beating, however sinful and shameful that might
appear, and the siren's pure wail interferes with the sullied night
on this side of the Sound.

Having passed through the cold of customs, the line of armed guards,
Having climbed the stairs to a meager heaven of currency,
I suddenly realized that I hadn't waved to a few who remained behind.

Even before the plane took off, they were forever transformed into shadows,
Echoes at the pit of the telephone, addresses in a half-forgotten little
    book,
And that is the only miracle of our time.

I knew that the voices would crumble and the words would turn into
    dust,
A familiar face would withdraw into the twilight of photographs,
While the bookshelves and lamps were finally crowding it out.

I didn't know who was Persephone's captive: I or they.
From the little table I looked at the level field through the glass:
The body I abandoned, as a poet from these parts once said.

There, next to the electric power station, the soaked sun will sag soon,
The tram cars will rustle, splashing mud on the March boulevards,
The ponds will thaw by Grand Georgian Street.

There, at some other time, near the many-windowed postwar wall,
A dead man lay face downward, the militia drove the people away,
And I didn't grasp at once what that signified.

Since that moment, I've been given enough time to understand:
Twelve, twenty, or even thirty years
In dark rooms, on vast and dark continents.

And, in the same place almost, a key squeaked in response to a knock,
And, in the same place almost, I learned how a line shines,
Illuminating the midnight trees and snow.

A country not one's own, entrusted like a temporary body,
The marshy land of the unvictorious, up to the Barents Sea,
The crosses of the airplanes above the invisible sky.

Bit by bit, at the edge of the unforeseen land,
Dreams change in the sultry weather,
And language will likely give way after them,
Since it also will not last forever.

In speech, no blackness of pines will be left,
No ravine of rough-faced fall,
Nor the wet and golden terrain of death,
Where the glacier knocks on the wall.

They retreat: the denouement, the swampy voices,
And, replete with untruth, the vastness,
And, disclaiming the voice, you listen close
To another body's distant darkness.

All night you listen to another blood's flow,
Where you live, as if in a mirror,
Where the heavy reflection leaves no glow
In the Neva or in the Neris.

*   *   *

I have learned to see in the dark, to distinguish happiness from
     happiness,
to understand what the closeness of another life can mean,
to grasp unexpectedly the changes in the time of year,
the way two or three atoms add weight to the air at noon.
The reflection in the window, vanished half a moment ago,
the voice mixed into the leaves, the breathing's scrambled traces
were repeating to me that you had returned to town before
a friend, a well-wisher, an enemy, God Himself was able
to say it. Like a Delphic fugitive, you hid
in the boles of cherry trees, elms, you changed, shifted the calendar,
having turned away from the ray, having turned almost into untruth
and nonexistence—that which is unable to grant him
even a drop of itself. Here the exchange is always uneven;
Phoebus is alive thanks to you, while you exist on your own
(what myth guesses, what Verbum and Logos have hidden,
we will grasp with ease, I think, when we cross the finish line)
and now, when the reflectors' echo thunders a double start,
when the concrete and wheels fly apart by a millimeter,
like a blizzard to one in Siberia, the name burns the throat,
the name that literally means snowy weather.
The wet curved mainland mirrors your features.
It's unclear whether stars are circling, or a wind is plunging,
and there's not much reality. The play of wind and waters,
the universe of clouds over Geneva, Varna, London.
Werther is already forgotten. All the places in the world
are marked in the diary. The word "I love" is erased.
The crash is much closer, even the homeland and the Lord
are closer than the body and soul just fifteen miles from this place.
There are no more signs in the sky, but still one can see and hear

in the final darkness, before the era of ice or fire.

It has been said that there will be no more time. Two thousand years, two drops, two airplanes roll through the hemisphere.

A Museum in Hobart

The country has been desolate for ages.
The pendulum of waves, the basalt's din.
We'll be more precise. A segment of the natives,
having survived three assaults on their kin,
signified nothing. Here's the cape, where later
they all turned into dust. A nomad folk,

naked and hungry. At the very edge,
which the poet sees involuntarily;
without a past. And almost without a speech.
Before last year, there was a skeleton here,
but they burned it—perhaps to show respect,
or take the space that it had claimed for years.

The place can't tolerate the void. I hear
space turn, I hear the breaches come together.
A new beginning overcomes this sphere
at the hands of several artists, rogues, tempters,
usually not too guilty. To be clear,
a British Gulag, modest in its scope,

which, later, in the deluge of nonbeing,
went under. Here is the globe's most peaceful place.
What happened, happened. "No" was spoken. Even
the tape recorder repents its mistakes,
and the autochthon menaces on the screen
good-naturedly, having returned from space

eternal: the low brow, inclining pate,
unwounded by the bloodstained clawlike thorns.

Today the powers' wardship would elate
even the dead. There language, you would own,
would be enriched as well—although, for that,
what's there to talk about within these zones?

Perhaps about how, on the line of time,
the prisons and the world are getting better.
A casino. Down by the stone circle,
the bronchi catch the wind, the sails glitter,
and he who finds the city a cozy home
does not return the ticket to the Creator,

nor to the Ansett Company. A hush.
A tribe without a feature or a trace.
Chains under the resistant glass. A grosz-
like history, worn underfoot, erased,
and, from the wreath of bay and ridge, the gush
of Antarctic mists, like ancient sea-spun lace.

This axe beside the roots. This rock. We are
no longer brothers, but neighbors anyway,
where time meets time like a perpendicular,
where our photographs and alphabets decay,
the splintered syllable, the ash and tar
still cry out something from the tourist display.

What is oblivion? Where is oblivion going?
Clepsidras trickle, baby rivers flow.
Along the crowded universe or nothing,

the lampshade sways, despair bursts into glow
at times. The sandstone slabs, a pier, the night,
signs on the wind. Drawings on the snow.

How late the cafés open,
And how fresh is the print of the damp newspaper!

Boris Pasternak

Before the middle of July, Paris
Is empty. Not a single phone replies,
Or else it answers in a borrowed voice,
Announcing that the number had changed somewhat
Since last year. The eloquent recording
Does not wish to reveal the latest cipher.
Why, you can't be so unaware by now,
We'll say, these things have ceased to be a secret:
Around the bend, the ruined Place des Vosges,
A winged courtyard genius, a balcony,
Unstable arches, propped with logs, just as
In Užupis. A sleepy laborer
Chisels the roadway. In the heated air,
A swallow draws the outline of a face
Retained in the memory just about as much
As any face. A motor has a coughing fit,
And then you hear a clank followed by curses.

The embankment stones are warm like honeycomb.
Acacia panicles in sidewalk cracks.
A cloud, as in a cutting in a forest.
Insane Tour Montparnasse. The midday, which,
To tell the truth, could not have come to pass.

"As I recall, a different emptiness
Was allotted you. You were required to grow

Up into it." The steps retreat on the square,
And the bell resounds on this side of the Seine.

"Will we have anything else to talk about?
Here are those same cafés, the soaring feathers,
Which you already knew before you saw them.
Most likely, they've been granted without a purpose.
You live inside the rupture of the map,
Inside the calendar."
                              Notre Dame's
Gray edge is not as far as I expected;
I see it beneath my feet, in the water, where,
Without rushing, it floats toward my side,
Having renounced the building.
                                        "I know
You're trying hard. But what is left for you?
The acoustics here are different."
                                        I was wrong,
This is not Notre Dame.
                              "By the way,
Soon even you will be transformed. The silence
In the receiver, chestnuts, glowing streets
Will perform this task for you. I know,
You will try everything. But then you'll tire.
The barracks in a hundred-mile morass,
The Black Marias, the squeaking boots, barbed wire
Will soon become a newspaper brevier,
A senseless flash in the circuits of consciousness,
Less real than even you, although
You're clearly lacking in reality."

The Bastille square, the colossal sun. It seems
I went against the current.
                              "I will add
Just one more detail: hope does not exist.
There's something more important than hope."

BERLIN SUBWAY. HALLESCHES TOR

Winter over Europe. The expanse of asphalted fields
Contracts, wrinkles, and splits like a chestnut shell.
The menacing pride of space is spent here. Winter
And the Berlin peninsula. A bone, cardboard, cement.

We see the sky inside out. There are guards on the streets.
A patch stands out on a wall, the blue lamps gleam.
A directionless void. The ball of thread will not lead
Out to alterexistence. Over Europe the snow flaps its wings.

You often don't know, after traveling years and miles,
Which shore you will meet. It's all the same, Jericho, Mitte—
The plans of the cities change, the termites toil,
And the trumpet will never give way to the voiceless whisper.

Turn around, and look from yesterday into tomorrow.
There, steeped in the dirtied snow, a man grows darker.
He's not destined to see a cardboard wagon crawl
Past Hallesches Tor, having been beyond nowhere and farther.

EAST ROCK

A beacon, barely visible from afar.
Two enormous boulders by the sea.
A little island, floating in the cove,
Resists the break of day without success.
It recedes, turning into a boat,
Then into a cherry pit. The sky filters
Through the clear cirrus. The flashes of the radar
Brush the axis of the earth at times.

The road has ended, there's nowhere to retreat.
Only space is visible through the gorge,
The cluster of trees tumbles down the banks,
A leaf quivers in the cemetery
Of air. Contours crumble, forms change,
And color meets up with its destiny,
Attaining the highest red inside the hewed
Cutting between October and September.

Watershed of months! Deadened senses
Of hornbeam groves, eloquence of bluejays!
The roaring pop of a motorcycle starting
At daybreak, five or seven blocks away!
By the cliff, curved like an elk's hide,
The grasses wither, the air becomes hoarfrosted,
So cold and so transparent, that it seems
To need our glance in no way whatsoever.

Today, slightly more clearly than today,
You identify the universe's blend:
It is born even before our birth,

Grows inside us from the primal cry,
Breaks through the fortress of the arteries,
Pierces the lungs and ripens in the lymph;
We have no sense that tells us this, except
The horror and darkness of the whole body.

The bluejay sings a short song over and over,
Changing the melody ever so slightly,
But there's no repetition and no change
For that which was given once upon a time,
So that, having united error with truth,
Destruction with passion, you would become a piece
Of the permafrost of your epoch, like the bones
In Kolyma, like stones past the Atlantic.

So then, take the shadow along with you,
The black mirror, the barren land of speech,
Choosing freedom every second, since
There is no other form of expiation.
Still the glass of water is not emptied,
Still no breeze has creaked the weather vane,
The car at the foot of the slope still does not know
If it will turn to the city, or to the north.

INSTRUCTION

The flight takes less than an hour. The border patrol
gives you no trouble; taking his time, he glances over the passport
(the only card in the never-ending game)
and waves his hand. Of course, a lot can change
in a year, a month or a minute;
there's a risk, albeit not great. Red brick slums
from the Mayerling epoch. A holiday. Portraits in the windows,
not seen for a good decade. Banners, slogans.
The best time in these parts; the authorities have cleared out of the city,
the archives are locked, the orderly is too lazy
to touch the disc with his finger; in all likelihood the prisons
have two or three watchmen left, those particularly in love
with their job. On such a day, the pilot,
not shot down, flies over the land where there's more uranium and
    steel
than grain; on such a day he lands in the city
to which you certainly won't return. True, he's braver.
November, dark boulevards; without fail, behind the arches, someone
is hiding, just as in a dream. All in all, this reminds one of a dream.

A hill in the mist, but there's no need to climb the hill.
Here, it seems, it is the only one. The flat plains stretch
to the Dnieper, then to the Urals and Gobi. Past the bridge, turn right.
The splendor of the blinded glass, the extinguished lamps,
the art nouveau fences, the old mosques will accompany you. There are
    few passersby.
You remain invisible to them. It's been drizzling for so many days.
A valley, a vast valley, like the bottom of a lagoon.
Stone snails above the doors; octopi and sea lilies

on the cornices; even the river is gray as a mollusk
that has crawled out of its shell.

It hasn't ended, and it won't end. A peasant-faced woman
is selling flowers. A carnation will do.
Here, already, it's not far. Usually the monument has guards,
whose duty it is to confiscate the flowers. But today is a holiday.
They, too, have a right to rest. Exactly thirty years ago,
on the square, there was a gathering (of a thousand? two? There would
    have been no room, probably, for five),
some with carnations, some probably empty-handed.
What happened afterward has been written in a wealth of books.
To read such books, you had to leave your homeland.
Here and there, perhaps, a split stone can be found,
a pockmarked stretch of granite, the corner of a building lopped off,
but after all these years you need a guide to help you grasp it.

You know little, to tell the truth, about the person on the square:
"having crossed his arms on the armor," "the walls of Jericho tumble
    down,"
"farther—farther—." Possibly the best verses on earth.
A Freemason, an artillerist. Lame, with a burned face.
Labiau, Ostrołęka, Wola, Temesvár.
There were somewhat more lost battles than won.
He died of fever in the town of Aleppo, soon after embracing Islam.

Not one passerby. Put the carnation at the feet,
so that the world may implode like a star, defeated by its own gravity.
The continent collapses into the valley, the valley into the city mist,

the city mist into the square, the square into the monument.
The carnation is the center of it all. Heavy, nothing but neutrons.
When you pass by, two hours later,
it will still be lying on the stone. Or, at least, so it will seem.

A meaningless gesture. You waited thirty years for it.
You changed countries, destinies, friends, but attained your end.
The people who then assembled on the square (not all of them returned
    home)
waited for a century. Even more: a hundred and eight years. What can
    you do:
these plains, steppes, mist teach you how to wait.

... a low dishonest decade ...
W. H. Auden

Summer submerges the city,
The glass reflects only dust,
Warm wine trickles
Into the hazy chalice.
The air is flavored with fading
Cupola gold in the sun.
Algae, like Cyrillic characters,
Blacken the narrow canal.

What do you seek here, poet?
An old balcony, a text
Effaced on the crumbling stucco,
The world, turned into dust.
The untied Gordian knot,
Lime, asphalt and tile,
The gateway mud, the litter
On stairways, the unclosed door.

Here, where gesture, life,
And sound once coincided,
The flowing crowds now speak
A slightly altered language.
The whiteness of June is throbbing,
And the blind brain, turning
To stone, no longer contains
All the time that was lost.

The new era colors the accent,
The syntax, the architecture,
The droplets of sun on the columns,
The bronzen smile in the bay.
Perhaps only poverty and hunger
Resist the era still,
Perhaps only shadow and fear
Linger on from our youth.

Grow accustomed to swimming in fear,
Just like a fish in the ocean.
Fear is long-lasting here,
Much more enduring than bodies.
Peaceful open squares
Are tasting the haze of noon.
Lime, asphalt, and tile,
Cyrillic on crumbling stucco.

Even now there remains of life
Several copper coins,
Time's change, counted out
By the local absurd bank.
Melody, gesture freeze over.
The prospect disclaims the alleys.
It's strange that we saw each other
Somewhat before we expected:

Not in the Vale of Jehoshaphat,
Not in the grove by Lethe,
Not even in the airless universe,

Where, in the manner of gods,
Kelvin and Becquerel rule.
The warmed wine is trickling.
Clouds of sleeplessness float
Over white and hot June.

The crowd and the sound float on,
But the weight of our craft stays the same:
To change time into a stanza,
To concentrate fear into meaning.
Only dust and the voice are throbbing.
The voice has no way of knowing
How much truth can fit
Into its shine and solitude.

in the fire in the fire in the fire in the fire in the fire
where space pulls over to the side and yields to time
cross out my soul make the not me in me expire
that the exalted nothing tasting peace may become
a spark a speck a line and a breach in the fire

in water in water in water in water in water
beneath the cupola filled with echo and ice
today you protect me and hand me out to others
may I not return home don't see me don't break my disguise
where eight bridges sway in the piercing cold in the water

underground underground underground underground underground
where the stone falls apart and the soundless stream stays together
where the winter matures and no color in green can be found
the body retreats into ash and ash into never
and from never to never the void flows under the ground

in the dark in the dark in the dark in the dark in the dark
our matter becomes dispersed and our air grows slack
all things are ready for death when the syllable sparks
and pressed into fictional paper the letters grow black
in this darkness here in this blindness here in this dark

* * *

After splashing the lips, the wave retreats into sudden
Refrain, regathering its force and essence. Immortality
Is just a sign, just a skill. The courtyards, the rubbing
Of bush against shutter, the melted candle repeat.

Like a stone in the water, the body dazzles the eyes,
The moths start to listen, the paraffin turns into steam.
We're drifting away from each other. I hear you glide
From paradise to death and paradise, from dream to dream,

To the breach between word and object. Now the whole of you
Is only what fingers remember. You'll vanish, I know,
And then return. Darkness reigns in the room,
And the bush starts to speak, and the pace of the sea grows slow.

Just a sign, a return. The gift of shadows and waves,
Signifying nothing, surpassing measure and line.
And the shutter squeaks, and the throbbing of speech and flame
Is eternity itself, blindly leaning on time.

* * *

An enormous book begins to flap like wings in the night:
Black, fire-embroidered Exodus, or a dictionary perhaps,
Ciphers, hieroglyphs, numbers . . . The meaning barred from our sight,
The thing not to be repeated by crystal, swallow, or grass.

Once heavily tilted, the stellar glory floats without direction,
The soul coincides with the century, the century is half-erased.
Time imprisons the soul and space is the body's deception,
And one can no longer draw the line between photo and maze.

Phosphorus, gold, and magnesium! Electric Tuscan sky!
The word loses its fullness, the shadow breaks from the sound.
Latin is dead, there are no singing discs here or on high,
Syntax has crumbled and scattered. Black soil, clay, and sand.

Perhaps only interjections and beats will sort this out.
We've tasted little honey, but lived what's worth living yet:
A garden, a spring, a stone . . . The brilliance of low-hanging clouds,
Nothing more sudden than existence and nothing more true than
    death.

Never ask why. Only he who pulled the door slightly ajar
To the place without hill or star, or certainty of grace,
Drives time away with a shield, like a fallen Etruscan at war,
Scoops up meaning in his hand, and washes his canceled face.

* * *

Half a mile away, where the highways cross,
A flame is struck up by a link of flint.
The ice, quivering above the springs, thaws,
And the reflection of the ash grove doesn't fit.

It's still too early for the bitterest stroke,
The banks will harden in transparent mist,
And even God, once simulating smoke,
Will dissipate. But that is not my gist.

Believe in winter. Drink the blessed cold.
Take pride in knowing that your home is lost.
Just like the ones who huddle in a boat,
Breathe darkness and the clarity of salt.

Sleep envelops Ithaca's hills and dales,
And injured children sleep without a quiver,
And only death will finally prevail,
And wet snow, and music, and nothing ever.

*　*　*

having unfolded a white burst of petals
a rose of the winds a grenade of snows with shattered rhombi
a rose of the winds with thorns of ice

In this city, weary
of saving humankind, where many cures
have been imposed upon the many nerves
of those who tell their sticky
dreams through shortened breath,
timed to the hour, softened
by sofas in the office,
where aging Europe's unbeloved
son conceived of death,

he who was so rashly
rejected by the artists' guild—today
the whirlpool swings the still boat into sway,
and the banks of the river swing
under the double range
of chestnut trees. In a café,
you hear the viral sputter of last year's rock,
and not ruins, but the ponderous baroque,
along with a star

stuck on the lofty balcony
bears witness to the arrogance of this land.
The rhythm rocks the consciousness to sleep.
The concave air at the square
slides into the eye—
so transparent, it seems
your feet swing like a pendulum,
and only music and pulse, in amalgam,
give you a hand.

You are blinded
by the color of the clouds; ambling
under arches; almost blended
with granite, dust, lilac blossoms,
you find no common words
with this euphonic chime;
too suddenly an outcast of your time,
not sure whether this is a curse
or a blessing.

Not straightening his back,
Sisyphus can rest
on the mountain's peak,
detaching his palm in terror
from the flaring stone —
the burden which for eons
wrecked him, then tamed him,
now stuck in gravel, aimless
and nameless.

It is sunny and still.
In the open, a dog rose spills
into blossom, and at last
there is no need to joust
with destiny,
rake the grass, stumble, slide
down the steep siliceous shoulder,
and youth slips, a moment later,
from your memory.

And if only one broken
sentence still disturbs the soul,
maybe these are just the strokes
of the taut bell "Bella
gerant . . . " And if at night
a wretched raft, about to be rolled
over by Austrus's rage,
is launched out into the sea,
others, not we,

will perish there. Blood fades;
a tank turns into dust.
An era has ended; the plague must
choose new lands. The train
no longer enters the terminal
where fire and space are fraternal,
where machine guns, speaking in Morse,
answer Moses and Christ
in snapping retorts.

The baroque celestial cloth
sinks over the Habsburg fortress.
Only beyond the horizon
where the air wounds, where a man
crawls into a hole, where stone
breaks into sand, where lead
so swiftly meets flesh, —between
Franz Ferdinand and today
there is no gulf.

The foliage, shattered
into splinters, like blackened plaster,
pastes up the mouth, and Saturn
is saturated with his sperm,
just as when time was first spawned.
And yet not here does torment
fuse late evening and dawn,
exceeding the terms
set forth for mortals.

In a camp, on a stone field,
refugees taste the darker
air of freedom, dreaming
visionless, having a few
happy hours to spend,
while those whom a bullet spent
(and saved) probably see starker
dreams, and yet seem stronger,
and more content.

Death is not here, she always looms.
The tones of the bells come closer;
she lives in granite, heat, wine,
and bread, in chestnuts entwined
with acacias. She roams
in dreams. History is part
of death. Galileo, not Hegel, was right:
eppur si muove. A dense, charred
sphere revolves into night.

What at first seemed real is just a denial
of time. There is no revival
in sleep. Nothing and clouds extend
through the window. Death
is not here. Death is at hand.
She rides around in the cage of the room,
crosses out the next calendar date,
then looks in the mirror and meets
you face to fate.

But while she still dallies in blackish glass air,
Sisyphus is needed here,
Here, in this insomniac city,
uninclined to distinguish the petty
from the things that matter, to unearth
the root of the foretold myth,
and await, without hope,
the trumpets of the Lord
on the diamond-sharp slope.

To Maurice Friedberg

A projector flickers in the somewhat cramped hall.
Only three viewers. Four, including one
who came from far away, who suggested this film
to his students. The oblong box preserves
a country where not even stones (or friends,
for that matter) remember him. Several languages
jostle in the subconscious. Garlands, faces,

and banners overcome the hanging blackness.
It's all unruly and festive. He who grew up
in a feastless state cannot bring himself
to look at the screen. He already knows
what's in store: dark warm bloodstains
and mud. No telling them apart, no telling
letters from fire, or truth from nothingness.

The heat drags down the university town.
Jasmines, fainting into a nod, surround
the ballast-covered paths and sweaty lawns,
where the water sprinkler fires away in series.
Distances grow. The newcomer tells his neighbor,
"But everything turned out well in the end—"
and tries hard to believe what he is saying.

AUTHOR'S NOTES

"Winter Dialogue": A poem about the Polish uprising of 1970. According to an old Lithuanian belief, one can establish the year of the uprising from the ring of the trunk of a tree, since the ring of the preceding year is very narrow.

"*Nel mezzo del cammin di nostra vita*": Konstantin Bogatyrev (1925–76), a poet and dissident, was murdered at the door of his Moscow apartment, presumably by the agents of the KGB.

"A Poem about Friends": On the 1968 demonstration in Red Square against the Soviet invasion into Czechoslovakia. "A hole in stone stairs" was made in the Lubyanka building in Moscow by the feet of many thousands of prisoners.

"Sheremetyevo, 1977": "A poet from these parts" is Fyodor Tyutchev.

"Instruction": On a visit to Budapest during the thirtieth anniversary of the 1956 Hungarian uprising (the date of the visit coincided with the anniversary of the October revolution). The quoted poem, by Cyprian Norwid, is dedicated to the nineteenth-century revolutionary Józef Bem. The events of 1956 started at Bem's monument.

"*Tu, Felix Austria*": "Bella gerant alii, tu, felix Austria, nubes" (Let others make war, you, happy Austria, make love), an old motto of the Austrian Empire.

A Dialogue
about a City

Czesław Miłosz and Tomas Venclova

Dear Tomas,

Two poets, one Lithuanian, the other Polish were raised in the same city. Surely that is reason enough for them to discuss their city, even in public. True, the city I knew belonged to Poland, was called Wilno, and its schools and university used the Polish language. Your city was the capital of the Lithuanian Soviet Socialist Republic, was called Vilnius, and you went through school and university in a different era—after the Second World War. Nevertheless, it is the same city; its architecture, its surrounding terrain, and its sky shaped us both. One cannot exclude certain, so to speak, tellurian influences. I have the impression that cities possess their own spirit or aura, and at times, walking the streets of Wilno, it seemed to me that I became physically aware of that aura.

Not long ago, a friend asked me why I persist in reminiscing about my memories of Wilno and Lithuania, which can be seen in my poems and works of prose. I replied that I didn't think it a matter of émigré sentimentality, since I had no wish to go there. Rather, it is a search for a reality purified by the passing of time, as in Proust; but there is still another interpretation. In Wilno, I spent my boyhood thinking that life would fall into place in the usual way, and it was only later that everything in that life was to turn upside down. So Wilno became for me an index of a possibility, the possibility of normalcy. Anyway, having read the Polish Romantics, I already had a hazy premonition of my impending and unusual misfortunes, but at that time even the most fertile imagination could not have envisioned my individual and the historic future.

Here I would like to introduce a character who has nothing in common with Wilno but is important for all Europeans who come "from over there"; that is, from that place which is the crossroads of languages, cultures, and beliefs. Stanisław Vincenz hailed from the

Subcarpathian Ukraine, near the range of Czarnohora, to which his family had emigrated in the seventeenth century from Provence. I met him in 1951 in France, near Grenoble, when my Wilno no longer existed. Even as an emigrant he was drawn to the mountains, thus bringing the wanderings of the Vincenz family full circle. I became receptive to his teachings. Apart from the writings he left us, Vincenz was a wandering sage, a talker, a teacher, something of a zaddik for people of various nationalities. He lived in opposition to the twentieth century even though—or actually because—he wrote his dissertation on Hegel before the First World War in Vienna. The most important thing for Vincenz was what Simone Weil termed *enracinement*, which is something impossible without a homeland. But the concept of a homeland-nation was too large, and when Vincenz dreamed of a "Europe of homelands," he had in mind small territorial parcels like his beloved "Huzul-land," populated with Ukrainians, Jews, and Poles, a small country famous, incidentally, because the Baal Shem Tov, the founder of Hasidism, had once lived there. At the time of our first conversations, I was very distressed, and Vincenz helped me discover the meaning of the word "homeland." I am not sure whether I would have written *The Issa Valley* several years later, as self-therapy, had it not been for those conversations, and like Vincenz, who spent his life rooted in his Carpathians, I, or my imagination at any rate, have remained true to Lithuania.

But let me get back to our extraordinary city. Perhaps we will be able to find continuity in it, despite the changes. We undoubtedly will turn our attention to the university where we both studied, about to celebrate its four hundredth anniversary. We also have an excellent opportunity to exchange our opinions about Polish-Lithuanian relations without constraint or the evasiveness of diplomacy.

Wilno cannot be excluded from the history of Polish culture if only because of Mickiewicz, the Philomaths,[2] Słowacki, and Piłsudski. I have often pondered the similarity between the Wilno of my youth and the Wilno of over one hundred years ago, which had the best university in the empire by the grace of Alexander I. At that time, it was a Masonic town. Actually, the defeat of the Philomaths coincided with one of Alexander's periodic attacks on the Freemasons throughout the empire. The Philomaths had their own Masonic connections through Kontrym, the university librarian. I knew of the existence of Masonic lodges in my newer Wilno, and the secret organization Pet, to which I belonged as a high school student, had its own ties with them. Politically, it was opposed to the Endeks.[3] When, not long ago, I met my former professor, Stanisław Świaniewicz, one of the youngest law professors we'd had, I learned that there had been many Masonic lodges, and that almost all the professors had belonged to one or another. In general, the Masonic character of Wilno described in his account (and he was an absolutely reliable source) astounded me. Whether one can deduce from this Wilno's abiding attributes, I do not know. At any rate, in school I chanced into something that resembled a "lodge" (I don't use this word in the literal sense but only to indicate a conspiracy of the elite to which one had to be admitted). That elite was contemptuous of "old-liners," of the whole complex: Polish nationalism, Sienkiewicz, student fraternities in their colorful caps. The Academic Vagabond Club, which I joined after entering the university, was such a "lodge." Somewhat later, during the large, albeit short-lived, swell of the left-wing wave in the early 1930s, I belonged to the I.C., or Intellectuals' Club, which was a coordinating cell for strategy planning as well as for arranging discussions in the headquarters of the Lawyers' Club for the law students. In these "lodges" I came to understand the meaning of the Romantic legacy—the dream of the salvation of mankind "from above" by those who "know better."

And the Right? Advocates of the slogan "God and Fatherland," "100 percent Polish"? Well, that's what the Polish-speaking majority was like. Linguistically, the old Wilno of the Philomaths must have been more Polish than the city I knew. I don't know whether the countryside was predominantly Polish-speaking, as it was in my day, or Belorussian. Perhaps then the Lithuanian language (as evidence in those areas gradually displaced by Belorussian) was entrenched closer to Wilno. The Russian-dominated nineteenth century also left its mark, and that is why I maintain that the old Wilno was probably more Polish. After all, almost half the population of my Wilno was Jewish, and a significant part of them adopted or gravitated toward Russian. That is why there were Russian-language high schools next to Polish ones in my Wilno. If I am not mistaken, there was a Hebrew school, and some Yiddish schools. (As you surely know, there was one Lithuanian high school named after Witold the Great, and a Belorussian one, too.) The Jewish intelligentsia, with their devotion to Russian culture, sent their children to the Russian schools because, after all, there weren't many Russians in Wilno, only the few that had stayed on from tsarist times, and a handful of immigrants. Other Russian influences remained, like that ugly Russian architecture peculiar to garrison towns, which presented so sharp a contrast to the narrow streets of the old city. The main street used to bear the name Świętojer-ski Prospect, and was still called "Jerek" in common parlance when I was a schoolboy. Jerek was a promenade, a place where gentlemen officers and students strolled. Later, we gradually became accustomed to its new name: Mickiewicz Street.

To compare Wilno with other cities is to bring out its specific character. The Psalmist called Jerusalem a city "enclosed within itself," and to a certain degree this description can be applied to Wilno, which sharply contrasts to cities built on a plain, like Warsaw. The compactness of Wilno reminds one of Kraków, but the layouts of the two cities are different, since Wilno does not have a town square to mark the center of the city. I have rather hazy memories of Dorpat or Tartu from childhood, and perhaps I am mistaken in supposing it has something in common with Wilno. Even in Czech Prague I felt a lot more "Wilno-ish" than in Warsaw. But historic Wilno was destroyed by fire so many times that perhaps it is simply its location at the confluence of two rivers, between the foothills, that gives the city its "compactness."

I felt quite strongly that Wilno was a provincial city rather than a capital; and had the territories that were ethnically Belorussian and Lithuanian been Polonized, it would have remained provincial. Let's look at France. The area south of the Loire was not French and langue d'oc was spoken there. From the time of the conquest in the thirteenth century, and under the pretext of the Crusades against the Albigensians, the area was gradually Frenchified. The whole countryside was still speaking patois in the nineteenth century, but when I was in the Department de Lot a few years ago, only the people over forty and living in small villages knew that language. The language was used by local Resistants during the war, and it was very useful because the city folk, that is, the French people, could not understand it. To put it in gross terms: had Poland not lost its historical stakes, all the land to the Dnieper would have been Polonized, just as France spread its language all the way to the Mediterranean Sea (and once Dante had thought of writing the *Divine Comedy* in the language of the poets, that is, langue d'oc!). Thus, Wilno would have been a regional city, like Carcassonne. But let's not get carried away with various historical "ifs." The program of the Polish Nationalists toward the non-Polish ethnic minorities in the twentieth century was stupid because Wilno and Lwów were enclaves. I think it is difficult for young people to understand the character of prewar Wilno as an enclave: it was neither

Polish nor not-Polish, neither Lithuanian nor not-Lithuanian, neither a provincial nor a capital city, although it was provincial above all. And really, as I see it in retrospect, Wilno was an oddity, a city of mixed-up, overlapping regions, like Trieste or Czerniowce.

Growing up there wasn't like growing up in places that were ethnically homogeneous, even language was felt differently. There was no popular idiom, country or city, with real Polish roots. There was a local language which was playful and closer in spirit to Belorussian than Polish. It incorporated many common Polish phrases from the sixteenth and seventeenth centuries that had fallen into disuse in Poland. The relationship between this "local" tongue and gentry Polish (the one that Mickiewicz heard in his childhood and later, with his "inner" ear, in Paris) is fluid, like that between the language of the gentry and the language of the manor, or the language of the intelligentsia derived from that of the manor. All of this was alien to the Polish peasant dialect. The Wilno proletariat spoke the "local" language, which did not represent the popular speech of Warsaw with its undoubted peasant substratum. For me, for example, the poet Miron Białoszewski is exotic; I don't share the same language resources. I would venture to say that our language was more susceptible to correctness as well as to a distinct rhythm; that is why we embraced as "our own" the clarified Polish of the eighteenth-century poets, such as Krasicki and Trembecki. It is a difficult thing to analyze. I would say that in my own case, my language was influenced by my resistance to the lure of the East Slavic languages—most importantly, Russian—and by the search for a register in which I could emulate the rhythmic modulation of the East Slavic elements. I do not know how the resistance to Russian affects your Lithuanian, but I know that for myself, and for everyone else who has an ear sensitive to Russian, yielding to the strong iambic "beat" of Russian is harmful, since it flows against the main current of the Polish language.

The provinciality of Wilno. It depressed me, and I longed to break away into the world. So I do not have to create a myth about a beloved, lost city since I could hardly bear it there. When the Wojewoda Bociański had me thrown out of the Polish Radio in Wilno as a political suspect, I accepted the forced exit to Warsaw with relief. Wilno was a backwater: an extremely limited place if you discount the Jews who spoke and read Russian or Yiddish and the local folk who read not at all. What was left? A few members of the intelligentsia of gentry background who were, in general, quite dense. This relates to the nationalism question; if we had considered ourselves to be Lithuanians, then Wilno would have been our capital and our center. It is a difficult problem, as you know. The logical solution would have been the Finnish one. I have no precise information on this subject, and I don't know how the Swedish-speaking Finns solved it, but Helsinki was probably their center, not Stockholm. In principle, we should have considered ourselves Polish-speaking Lithuanians and under new conditions continued with Mickiewicz's "Oh Lithuania, my native land." This would have meant the creation of a Lithuanian literature in the Polish language on a par with a Lithuanian literature in the Lithuanian language. Of course, no one wanted this—neither the Lithuanians who bristled defensively against Polish culture as denationalizing, nor those who spoke Polish and considered themselves Poles and behaved contemptuously toward the Klausiuks, a nation of peasants. Individuals with different ideas were few, although very interesting, valuable, and energetic. In my Wilno, there was a group known as *krajowcy*, or Regionalists, who dreamed of maintaining the traditions of the Grand Duchy of Lithuania as the only counterbalance to Russia or of forming a federation of nations established on the order of the Grand Duchy. This group of Regionalists more or less coincided with the milieu of Wilno Freemasons. The history of this singular ideology should be written someday, but if I say that it is interesting—even fascinating—then I am saying it ex post facto, because as a young man with a passion for the avant-garde, contemporary poetry, the French intellectual movement, etc., I was not interested in what was close by and demanded greater attention. Besides, it was a movement that had already been defeated and whose last echoes had been heard. From the Lithuanian camp there wasn't a shred of sympathy for it because it represented a prolongation of the "Jagiełłonian idea." Undoubtedly, underneath the sentimental attachment to the idea of the Grand Duchy, the dream of domination lay hidden within some of the gentry descendants. All the same, Ludwik Abramowicz and a few other Regionalists were intelligent people who were sincere in their resistance to Polish nationalism. These men were the inheritors of broad thinking comparable to that of the enlightened people in the eighteenth-century Republic. I do not think there was an equivalent movement on the Lithuanian side—only the new nationalism, which was by nature spasmodic. Whichever way you look at it, only the Polish-speaking Regionalists from Wilno regarded Wilno as a capital and not a province. Now I think that anyone who wishes the city well would want it to be a capital, and that would automatically remove Poland's claim to a "Polish Wilno."

At this juncture I must raise the question of national treason. As you know, where there are painful feelings, it is easy to blame; no doubt you have experienced this yourself. The Regionalist idea was subject to the accusation of "treason" from both the Polish and Lithuanian nationalists. This brings to mind many instances: once in 1967 I was in Montreal for the Rencontre Mondiale de Poésie with Adam

Ważyk. We found ourselves with a group of Quebec intellectuals full of French fanaticism. Also, several years later when I took part in a poetry conference in Rotterdam, I met a lot of Flemish-speaking Belgians who preferred English to French and, of course, spoke English better than French. Before the war, during my year as a student in Paris, my visits to Oscar Miłosz at the Lithuanian Mission smacked of "treason." To the Poles, Oscar Miłosz was a "traitor," and I observed how such hostility moves like an electric current, virtually without words. In these matters a community has its own secret ways of understanding itself. The letters of Oscar Miłosz to Christian Gauss, which I discovered in the Princeton Library and published in a separate volume in Paris, answered the questions of "how" and "why" he declared himself a Lithuanian. When he did so in 1918, he knew nothing of the Lithuanian national movement and became angered when he discovered that the Poles refused to acknowledge Lithuania's independence. (This was the attitude of the nationalistic Poles, the followers of Dmowski who were serving as diplomats during the Peace Conference.) Subsequently, he worked on behalf of Lithuania in the international forum. In retrospect, one can see that his position on Wilno was correct. Nonetheless, although the Lithuanians respected him, they mistrusted him because he wasn't a speaker of Lithuanian, only Polish. (Actually, he spoke French, and that is why he could make a choice.) If I had declared myself a Lithuanian, what kind of Lithuanian would I be, writing in Polish? That mistrust of Oscar Miłosz was the reason for his voluntary resignation from a diplomatic career and his acceptance of a modest position as counselor at the mission, although he had been offered the position of minister of foreign affairs. Witness, on the other hand, the vindictiveness of the Poles. When in Poland Arthur Międzyrzecki translated Oscar Miłosz's novel *L'Amoreuse Initiation* and Oscar's oeuvre was discussed, a letter to the editor appeared in *Tygodnik Powszechny* reminding the readers that Oscar Miłosz had nothing in common with Polishness because he had renounced it.

There were some attacks against me in the Lithuanian émigré press because, even though I am a relative of Oscar Miłosz, I am a Pole, not a Lithuanian. On the other hand, I was often suspect among Poles who thought that there was something amiss with my Polishness. I must admit that there was some faint reason for this, although as a child in Russia, I used to recite the ditty: "Kto ty jestés? Polak mały. Jaki znak twój? Orzeł biały." (Who are you? A little Pole. What's your emblem? The White Eagle.) In Russia and in the presence of Russians, I always felt 100 percent Polish (that was easy!). My conflict with the ethnically rooted Poles from the Congress Kingdom of Poland is something else.

My relations with Poland were no less, perhaps even more, painful than Gombrowicz's. But it would be an exaggeration to infer from this a gravitation toward Lithuania when, in fact, it was my avoidance of total participation in any kind of human community that was deciding my personal fate, my burden, my affliction. But one must also see in this my conflict with the prewar Polish intelligentsia because my mentality was much more international and cosmopolitan.

It is difficult to recall all of this now. Various things influenced me during my school years, such as the literary journals that were not the organs of the Polish intelligentsia but of the Polish-Jewish intelligentsia. I refer here to the Warsaw journals such as *Wiadomości Literackie*. Hence, perhaps, my early rebellion against Sienkiewicz and the Polish Soul—which was the *anima naturaliter endeciana.*[4] Then in my student years there was the influence of Oscar Miłosz. In his political works (issued posthumously) one can find a very sober analysis of the situation. In 1927 he wrote that Poland might have been able to forge a block around itself via tight alliances of the Baltic nations, Finland, and Czechoslovakia so as to create a counterforce to German pressure. But for this to occur, Poland would have had to renounce its *messianisme national outrecuidant et chimerique,* which it could not do, so that some ten years later it reached the point of catastrophe.

I must tell you of yet another influence on my life, and this will be a long tale. You are not my first Lithuanian friend. In my student years I had another Lithuanian friend who affected me deeply. He was not from Wilno but from—as they used to say—"Kaunas Lithuania." How did he come to us? As you know, diplomatic relations between Poland and Lithuania during my university years, 1929–34, did not exist. The border was closed, and both sides played tricks on each other. Poland financially subsidized "Polishness" in Lithuania, and Lithuania did the same for "Lithuanianness" in the region around Wilno. I met him in 1929, in a proseminar on philosophy of law taught by Professor Ejnik: suddenly a tall fellow with tousled hair and horn-rimmed glasses took the floor and tried to speak Polish, but it was actually Russian laced with German. His name was Pranas Ancevičius or Franciszek Ancewicz, and here is his very sad story. He came from a poor peasant family, got into high school, became fascinated with revolutionary Russian literature (Gorky, etc.), and became a revolutionary. He took part in an unsuccessful socialist coup in 1926 and had to flee Lithuania. He escaped to Vienna, where he lived in a working-class housing complex named in honor of Karl Marx. There socialists helped him out. In general, Pranas, or Draugas[5] as I called him, was to remain a radical socialist all his life in the style of Viennese Marxism. Therein lies his tragedy. No doubt he was a person with a yearning for political activity but condemned to the fate of an emigrant. He was considered "out" by the local Lithuanians in Wilno because they were loyal to the

Kaunas government and he was a political criminal. In turn, the Lithuanian communists thoroughly hated him because he irritated them with his excellent knowledge of Soviet affairs, on which he bluntly expressed his opinions. Exercising their usual practice of slander, they declared him a "Polish agent," "provocateur," etc. They spread rumors that he was bought and paid for; how else could he get money for his studies? I lived with Draugas on the same floor of the dormitory on Bouffal Hill, and I knew that the modest income he lived on (and Wilno was an unusually cheap city) came from America and, no less, from the anticlerical and leftist Lithuanian press, for which he was a correspondent (he was a passionate atheist). When his money came late, Draugas lived on credit. I was also a witness to his deep and long-lasting depressions, his great talents having been coupled with severe neurosis. So the outcome of my conversations with Pranas (notice that they occurred during my formative years) explains why I knew ten times more about communism when I moved to Warsaw than all of my literary colleagues put together, because Pranas kept track of everything that was happening beyond the eastern border. Obviously my perspective on Poland and Polishness, which was by nature Endek-like and parochial, was transformed by his training.

I do not want to exaggerate my politicization. I was not suited to any political commitment or involvement, for which I reproached myself, but I never knew how to conquer my individualism and accept organizational discipline. Pranas was the president of the ZNMS (Association of Independent Socialist Youth) at the university, but I never joined this organization, and while his friendship was one thing for me, his revolutionary beliefs were another.

Pranas received his doctorate in law and began to lecture at the Institute for East European Research. This is a good time to touch on a few subjects that are certainly still enigmatic today, such as the inconsistent Polish policy toward Lithuanians, Belorussians, and Ukrainians. The fact is that, as we similarly witness in America, various forces conflicted with one another in Poland, although, with each consecutive year of the 1930s, the Right, with its Polonization program, grew stronger through the use of police tactics, culminating in the brutal pacification of the Ukrainian countryside. In Wilno, the harassment of the Lithuanians was left to the Wojewoda Bociański, after Piłsudski's death. At the same time, the Institute for East European Research was created and established by completely different forces, which were being pushed out by a belligerent nationalism with fascistic stubbornness. These forces could be described as liberal, not without Masonic ties, and adhering to Piłsudski's federalist dreams. They were not all socialists or Masons; Świaniewicz, for instance, was in the institute (as were a number of professors from the Stefan Batory University), and he was an ardent Catholic all his life.

There came a time when the provincial administration began forcibly deporting certain Lithuanians, literally throwing them across the border into Lithuania. They wanted to deport Pranas, and in Kaunas they would of course have jailed him. But it was the people from the institute who defended him. The concept of establishing the institute was undeniably an excellent one; I don't know about elsewhere, but certainly in Poland there was an obligation to study one's neighbors. At the very least those people who were preparing to serve in the administration and diplomatic corps should have been obliged to do so! The institute taught what is today referred to as Sovietology many years earlier than that branch of learning was developed in America. It offered the economics, geography, and politics of the Soviet Union as well as the languages of our area: Lithuanian, Estonian, Latvian, and Belorussian. It was significant that when in Wilno, the ex-members of our poetry group, Żagary, Henryk Dembiński, and Stefan Jędrychowski were accused of being communists, and even when, a little later, they were convicted in court, those circumstances did not prevent the administration of the institute from hiring them. The secretary of the institute was my fellow poet, Tadeusz Bujnicki. Stefan Baczyński (father of the poet Krzysztof Baczyński) commuted from Warsaw to lecture. Baczyński was very left-wing and quite typical of a certain kind of mentality: a Piłsudski-ite, a legionnaire, a participant in the Polish uprising in Silesia, he came from that segment of the Polish intelligentsia which fought for an independent Poland in the name of its radical ideas. It seems to me that Pranas Ancevičius and Baczyński took a liking to one another, and that Baczyński persuaded Pranas to move to Warsaw, far from the local government. He also helped him find a job—I don't remember whether it was in a research institute or a library; at any rate, it was before the war broke out.

In my student days Wilno was everything adjacent to Cathedral Square: on one side, the university; on the other, at the corner of Mickiewicz Street, Rudnicki's Café, and next to it, the Institute for East European Research. At our university we felt continuity more than at other Polish universities (with the possible exception of the Jagiełłonian). It was as if the period of its closing (after the Uprising of 1831) somehow had contracted and disappeared, and again one found oneself in the aura of the Philomaths. Growing up in Wilno meant that one belonged to the twentieth century in a limited way only, probably owing to the cinema. Today, I sometimes confuse the Academic Vagabond Club, especially the Club of Senior Vagabonds, with the Society of Scoundrels founded by the professors of the young Mickiewicz. Even the lodge named the Zealous Lithuanian, it seems, continued to flourish in my student years.

In comparison with Wilno, Warsaw was an ugly city, corroded in its inner districts and certain suburbs by extreme poverty—either the

Jewish poverty of cottage industries and small merchants, or the Polish one, proletarian. It simply could not measure up to civilized cities like the Czechs' beautiful Prague. Nevertheless, Warsaw represented the twentieth century. For the newly arrived from Warsaw (like K. I. Gałczyński), Wilno was total exotica. But Warsaw disturbed me. Midway through my law studies I transferred for a year to the University of Warsaw, and that was a bad experience. I flunked my exams (with professors who could not compare to those in Wilno), and I returned to Wilno.

To this day I cannot answer the question why I wasted so much time studying law. It was like this: I started out in Polish language and literature, which I dropped after two weeks, and from the moment I signed on to law, a stupid stubbornness (Lithuanian?) or the shame of quitting forced me to finish the degree. Law was at that time a good general education, as is anthropology or sociology today in America. Those who did not know what to do with themselves studied law. The humanities obliged you to say to yourself: "Well, I suppose I'll be a teacher in a grade school." In youth, one has those lofty and undefined dreams; it's difficult to be realistic and choose a modest career in teaching. Today, knowing what I know, I would not pick Polish literature or philosophy (I attended lectures and seminars in philosophy), but the classics, and I would also have studied Hebrew and the Bible. At that time, however, the study of Latin and Greek was a prescribed traditional program that consisted mainly of reading the ancient poets, and the Greek tragedies, for example, read from professorial translations, bored me to tears. I had had enough Virgil in school, and I found all of philology deadly dull. Today, Latin and Greek (which I began to study after the age of sixty) represent something entirely different to me: access to the world of Hellenism and the beginning of Christianity. If I had found someone intelligent to guide me, perhaps I would have slogged through the boredom. There was one good professor of Greek, Stefan Srebrny, with whom I should have studied. And if I had learned Hebrew, then I would have been one of the few well-educated men of literature . . . Nonetheless, and in my opinion, law in Wilno was better than at other Polish universities, because during each of the four years required for the degree we had at least one course that was truly inspiring. In this group I would include the following: Theory of Law (Professor Ejnik); Constitutional History of the Grand Duchy (Iwo Jaworski); Criminal Law (Bronisław Wróblewski, who actually taught a course in anthropology under that pretext); and the History of the Philosophy of Law (Wiktor Sukiennicki). Thus in Wilno, in grade school and at the university, I received a very decent education, but it could have been better. We must take into consideration that after 1918 the educational system suddenly had to be improvised, and there was no dearth of people who found themselves in the faculties by sheer accident. At any rate, there wasn't a professor in Wilno who was as disreputable as the notorious Jarra in Warsaw, who forced students to memorize his handbook on the theory of law for exams and flunked students who responded "in their own words." (While, as a matter of fact, his handbook was just plain gibberish.)

In talking of Wilno it is important to mention that it was significantly a Jewish city. In a way completely different from Warsaw. The Jewish quarter in Wilno was a labyrinth of utterly medieval, narrow streets, houses connected by arcades, and rough pavements two or three meters wide, while in Warsaw there were those hideous streets of nineteenth-century tenement houses! The poverty of the Jews was less noticeable in Wilno, which doesn't mean that it didn't exist. But that doesn't account for the difference between the two cities. Wilno was a stronghold of Jewish culture and had a long tradition of being such. I must point out that it was precisely here, on this working-class, Yiddish-speaking, Jewish foundation, that the prewar Bund was formed. Its leaders, Alter and Erlich, were later shot by Stalin. Wilno had a Jewish Historical Institute, which was later moved to New York. I think that Wilno especially contributed to the rebirth of Hebraism in Israel. Having lived in such a city, I should have gained some knowledge of all this, but custom was the obstacle. Jewish and non-Jewish Wilno lived separately. They also did not write or speak the same language. As a student, I was internationally inclined, though this interest was quite shallow and I knew nothing of the history of the Jews in Poland and Lithuania, nor of their religious ideas, their mysticism, the Cabbala. It was only much later, in America, that I was to learn about these things. This gives you some idea of the separation of the two communities; but what is the use of talking about other cities in prewar Poland when I, in such surroundings, was an ignoramus? No one in Poland, as far as I know, dared to propose that Hebrew be taught as one of the classical languages, or that the intellectual history of the Polish Jews be taught, or even that the Old Testament be read and discussed: he would have been stoned. And if the hatred of the Jews toward the Poles, in view of their extraordinary forgiveness of the Germans and Russians, deeply disturbs and hurts me, I must admit that petty anti-Semitism gets under the skin just as much as crime because it is an everyday occurrence.

I hope that you will find material for reflection in my letter. You and I want Polish-Lithuanian relations to develop differently from those of the past. The two nations have terrible experiences behind them; they were defeated, humiliated, and downtrodden. New generations will talk to each other differently from the way they did before the war. We have to reckon with the force of inertia and also the fact that in the ideological void that has come about, nationalism, whether in Poland or Lithuania, will at times fall back into worn tracks. As in the history of every country, repetitious patterns persist. At the end of the eighteenth century, there was a schism between the Reform and Sarmatian° camps, and this break, under various guises, has remained to this day; however, in its covert or semicovert state, it defies definition. It is possible that Adam Michnik's book, *The Church, the Left, and Dialogue* (published by Kultura in Paris), heralds the end of this schism. For in our century it was the Church that, at least until 1939, served as the mainstay of the Sarmatian mentality, which engendered modern-day nationalism. A new union is being formed; great energies of progress are igniting within the Polish Church, and in the present regime such progress can only mean the effective defense of the human individual. But these are complex changes, not day-to-day ones, and they do not necessarily signify the disappearance of prewar nationalistic attitudes, which a significant part of the clergy has retained.

The Lithuanians in the years 1918–39 despised everything that I held dear in Wilno: regionalism, the federalist dreams, the Regionalists, and the liberal Freemasons who supported Piłsudski. Evidently, the Lithuanians preferred to deal with the *anima naturaliter endeciana* because at least then their enemy was clearly defined. Perhaps they were right; it is not for me to judge. And so it is this Regionalist concept, not the Sarmatian one, that gives hope for the friendship between Poles and Lithuanians today. And finally, it is precisely this idea which is the political legacy of Jerzy Giedroyc, editor of Paris *Kultura*, with which I have been associated for many years.

Dear Czesław,

I left Vilnius a year and a half ago, and I don't know whether I'll ever return to that city — at any rate, not in the near future. One of my friends, also a recent émigré and an ambitious Sovietologist, claims that enormous changes could take place in Eastern Europe within literally a few years. In such a case our emigration would end naturally. Although I tend to be an optimist, I don't agree with his viewpoint. The situation there will no doubt go on indefinitely, and we must grow accustomed to this other life in the West. In a way it is life after death. We meet people whom we had no hope of meeting on this earth, and we may be separated from our old friends forever. Contact with them has a sort of spiritualistic quality, and as the old landscapes grow remote, we begin to see clearly what was once only a haze. I am writing this from a little hotel in Venice a few steps away from San Marco, and if someone had suggested to me five years ago that I would be here conversing with you in writing, I would have responded that he had an incredibly wild imagination.

I still remember each alley in Vilnius. I could walk through that city blindfolded, wrapped in my own thoughts, and find my way. Occasionally I do this in my sleep, but it is slipping away from me, never to return. I know that Vilnius is changing and that I will not take part in these changes. I am beginning to see the city in a simpler, general, perhaps more historical way. I don't admit to nostalgia. When I decided to emigrate, many people told me that nostalgia is a terrible thing: I told them that I agreed, but that it could not be any worse than the great longing I was feeling for France, and Italy, etc. I am happy to hear the bells of Venice, and to know that in five minutes I can see San Giorgio Maggiore again — perhaps the most beautiful facade in the world. I wouldn't want to return to present-day Vilnius, and to tell you the truth, I couldn't stand it there. Nonetheless, I like the city, and only now am I beginning to understand that it also is a part of Europe.

We do not know the same Wilno or Vilnius. As a matter of fact, we can say that they are two extremely different cities. Such a complete transformation is not a common occurrence. I think Warsaw changed less, despite its having been totally destroyed. Perhaps more analogous to Vilnius's fate is that of Gdańsk, or Wrocław (or even worse yet, Königsberg). In those places, the people, the language, and types of civilization changed completely. Vilnius, like Gdańsk (which had Polish environs and certain Polish substratum), belonged to historical Lithuania, but was also close to ethnographic Lithuania. Still, everything is new now. What remains the same is the sky, the river Wilia (now called the Neris), and even the sandy shoals in that spot where the Wileńka (now Vilnelė) flows into the Wilia. Some trees, many trees remain, but what else? Oh yes, the architecture has remained, and this is important.

I think architecture gives cities their aura; all other things, such as lifestyle, even landscape and climate in a certain sense, are derived from it. Vilnius is a Baroque city. The Baroque, in general, demands space, distance, and perspectives; cities of the Baroque epoch are laid out in the modern way. The Vilnius Baroque is Baroque against a medieval background, the network of the streets is medieval—everything there is crooked, narrow, tight, and tangled. Above this labyrinth rise the mighty cupolas and towers of an entirely different century. Nothing there appears whole: parts of churches, slanting walls, and halved silhouettes loom up from around each corner. From musty and dirty alleys, the grand, white bell tower of St. John's suddenly shoots up into the sky, or a small classical square is revealed. The history and the human dimension of the city—it's the same sort of maze. Of course, you know this well. When I was a schoolboy, half of this Vilnius stood in ruins, yet all the churches by some miracle survived. Artillery fire ruined one of the two lovely towers of St. Catherine's, which was rebuilt later on. Of course, the Soviet officials closed the majority of the churches and turned them into warehouses for paper and vodka. Later, with varying degrees of success, some churches were converted into museums. Nonetheless, the outward appearance remained intact. The city merges with its setting: on a clear day one can see the lines of pediments reflecting the line of the surrounding wooded hills—or perhaps vice versa. You once wrote that even the clouds over this city are Baroque. They are.

I don't want to dwell on this Baroque. Vilnius has all the European styles with the exception of the Romanesque, and they are of good quality. The mixture is really quite strange, but the styles coexist in a very effective way.

During my school years I was seriously interested in this architecture. Not only was I familiar with all of Vilnius's monuments, but I knew just about every window and column. I acquired more knowledge of architecture than of the other arts, and I cultivated my visual and spatial imagination (unfortunately I lacked a musical one). I had several friends with the same flair for architecture, and we would amuse ourselves for hours, guessing styles, centuries, even decades, and enumerating Vilnius's curios from memory. A book published in 1940 by Mikołaj Worobiow was a great help to us. Professor Worobiow emigrated to the States after the war, where he committed suicide. (I unexpectedly met his lovely daughter, who lives in New York City, the day after I arrived there.) His book, published only in Lithuanian, is something of a Wilnoesque Ruskin or Muratov. Later, after I had visited many cities, the "Vilnius sickness" passed somewhat. However, I must admit that during the worst times in my adult life, I would walk to the Skarga courtyard, or to the little square in front of St.

Anne's, or in front of St. Teresa's, I would stand and gaze, and it always helped.

Now I am experiencing something similar in Italy. Topographically Vilnius is very like Rome. It even has (just as Rome does) a layer of pagan antiquity. Here I would like to mention a little story. Before the war a group of Lithuanian students went on a tour of Europe. One of the participants described this excursion eloquently: "We arrived in Florence: the city is nice, similar to Vilnius, except that it is worse." The funny thing is that I agree almost completely. Vilnius belongs to the same world as does Florence. Russia is completely different, perhaps with the exception of St. Petersburg, but St. Petersburg is a complex issue. Cities such as Tallinn or Tartu, in my opinion, have little in common with Vilnius except for their unfortunate fate. They belong to Europe within the Scandinavian sphere.

Quite early on, I began to perceive the architecture of Vilnius as a sign. It made a statement and exacted a demand. It was the proud past in the midst of the strange and uncertain present; a tradition in a world suddenly torn away from tradition; a culture in an acultural world. The culture—why hide it?—was to a significant degree Polish. It was also Italian, German, and French, but Christian above all (which I understood later). You say that for you Wilno held the possibility of normalcy. For me that normalcy never existed. During my childhood I had a strong, although vague, sense that the world was twisted, turned inside out, and maimed. Later, I began to think, and I do to this day, that we are living after the end of the world, which does not incidentally absolve us from any responsibility. In my Vilnius, only the enclaves gave some semblance of that lost, normal world. Of course, normalcy is something relative, and I suspect that human existence doesn't ever fall into place in the usual way. Everyone dreams about ordinariness now and then, but ordinariness was always a sort of ideal average not coincident with facts. In our time the most unbelievable misfortunes are perhaps the most frequent and, therefore, the most ordinary.

Recently I read Thomas Mann's essay, "Lübeck as a Way of Life and Thought." In it he writes about a peaceful, dignified world, always striving for a middle way. Important in that world are such categories as reason, responsibility, and home. Certainly this has changed. These categories are no longer handed down to us "from the beginning" by tradition; they can, and can only, be a mission. This means, we must grow up to a sense of responsibility, to a reasonable and dignified life, to some unmechanized place of our own, if not in space then in time. It is a maturity achieved with difficulty, with constant apprehension of losing. This is the result, above all, of the totalitarianisms of the twentieth century. One of these totalitarianisms appeared in the well-ordered fatherland of Thomas Mann, but that is a separate issue.

I don't come from Vilnius. I was born in Klaipėda, which my parents were forced to leave in 1939 when Hitler took over the city and its environs. I was two years old at the time. I spent my childhood— or rather, I should say, the German occupation—in Kaunas. Later I became a Vilniusite, like thousands of other Lithuanians who, during and after the war, came to their historic capital. It was a city complete-ly unknown to them. Before the war, contact between Wilno and independent Lithuania virtually did not exist. There was instead the myth of Vilnius with its importance for the Lithuanian imagination, about which I will say something later, but that belongs to a different dimension of things. There were, and still are, Lithuanian natives of Vilnius, who are an interesting, if small, group of people, now dying out. Life in Vilnius from the beginning was a difficult adjustment to a new soil. What's more, there was general chaos.

As I mentioned before, half of the city was in ruins. On the old

Jerek every other house was burned down. That old wooden movie house, Helios, remained intact (now the rather pretentious Vilnius Opera stands more or less in the place where it used to be). The vicissitudes of the name of this street deserve a separate account. The Lithuanian authorities changed its name to Gediminas Street, leaving the extension to the suburb of Zwierzyniec as Mickiewicz Street. Somewhere around 1950, it was announced that in deference to the working class, it would be named the Comrade Stalin Prospect. It bore this lofty name until the Twentieth Party Congress. At that time, one of my friends, a novice graphic artist, wrote a petition to the officials proposing the name revert to its original. He was summarily dismissed from school and, in accordance with the old custom, found himself a recruit in the Red Army, from which he returned a broken man. He later did manage to work at his profession, but he became ill and died. (It was rumored that his death was the result of the strong exposure to radioactivity, which he had received at a northern army base.) Finally, the street became—of course—Lenin Prospect, but my generation always referred to it as Gediminka. It must be pointed out that officially the name Gediminas was retained because it was given to Cathedral Square. Thus, religion was erased from the map, and Lithuanian nationalism, although not completely eliminated, was put in the place where it belonged; that is, second.

The entire ghetto, as well as German Street (whose name was immediately changed to Museum Street), was an eerie and lifeless area that probably resembled postwar Warsaw. Although the walls of the old synagogue were still standing, the whole thing was demolished without delay. Several other objects that were not entirely acceptable to the new order were also razed. One morning we noticed that the Three Crosses[5] had disappeared—blown up during the night. Then the three holy figures were taken off the pediment of the cathedral.

The press reported that they were not in the original Stuoka Gucewicz⁹ project, which was the truth, except that the cross in the original project was also removed. Rumors were tossed about that a highway would be built connecting the train station with the Antakalnis (Antokol) district and, of course, Ostra Brama¹⁰ and two churches, the Dominican and St. Catherine's, stood in the path of this proposed project. There was talk of replacing St. Jacob's with an authentic Soviet-style skyscraper on the Lukiškės (a similar skyscraper had been built in Riga). After Stalin's death these beautiful projects were somehow forgotten. But the whole city was surrounded by gray, standardized housing, which made the garrison architecture of tsarist times appear quite decent. These houses effectively ruined the Antakalnis district and began to encroach into the historic center, right up to Museum Street.

My school, a former Jesuit high school, stood at the end of this street, looming up as a sort of island among the ruins. It was a large and very bleak building, and the memories I carried out from it are not the best. The various crises of my youth coincided with the aforementioned feelings of abnormality, and of a distorted world. On the first day of school, I got lost in the ruins, and that exhausting, helpless, four-hour roaming in search of my house (I could not ask directions home because the few people I met did not speak Lithuanian) became a private symbol for me. The Vilnius population in that early period was not very large, and besides they were an extremely strange bunch. Practically all the Jews had perished; the Poles were moving to Poland en masse (or to Siberia), and what remained was the proletariat— mainly lumpen. The Lithuanians belonged either to the new Soviet elite or to the survivors of the old intelligentsia, and were often broken or intimidated. A number of Russians appeared on the scene, as well as other immigrants—functionaries and occupation officers with beautiful daughters. There were also a good many Russian people eking out an existence by begging, or worse. From the "local" Russian and fragmented Lithuanian population a new and strange jargon arose. The city was full of criminals and dangerous. Often fights would break out, usually under the pretext of settling some ethnic score. Above all, one felt the heavy hand of authority.

Of course, I reacted to all of this differently from the majority because my family was part of the Soviet elite; nevertheless, I felt it. Able to take advantage of my father's rich library, I became interested in many things. In time, I became aware of the fact that some names and problems were nonexistent because it was forbidden to mention them. This irritated and humiliated me. In several books—and these were books of Greek literature—the name of the translator had been erased. I asked my father what this meant, and he answered that the books had been purchased from a Moscow antiquarian and that he didn't know anything more about the translator. Sometime later I learned that he was Adrian Piotrowski (the son of the famous classical scholar Tadeusz Zieliński), who died in the Stalinist purges. Another translator of Greek classical literature (this time into Lithuanian) also could not be mentioned because he was Smetona, the former president of independent Lithuania. But what's the use of mentioning Smetona when over half of all Lithuanian literature didn't exist because it was considered evil and inimical? Later I understood that it was the same for Russian literature. Neither the problem of nationality nor of religion existed; therefore, with the passage of time, both aroused my curiosity. Most of the countries in the world didn't exist either. For me, France and England were literary concepts something like Jules Verne's islands, as was Poland. These countries were either pure fantasy or at best represented the past; in the present there remained a sort of undifferentiated (because it was the enemy's) and absolutely inaccessible expanse. Later, after I had finished the university, I came across a copy of a book called *Everything about Wilno in 1913*. On the first page there was a long list of foreign cities to which one could buy a direct train ticket from Wilno. I wondered to how many of these cities a ticket could be bought now: I found only two—Lwów and Königsberg.

Everything was done to eradicate the past and implant a new mentality. It's clear that it wasn't just a matter of the desecration of crosses or the fact that theaters which had been named Casino and Adria became Moscow and October (which they are called to this day). The new ideology was forcibly imposed in every possible way, especially to humiliate and emphasize the worthlessness of the individual. The older schoolteachers and university professors, gagging with helpless rage, said things they didn't believe and about which no human being should have talked. The poet Putinas, already on in years and universally acclaimed, was silent for a time, but then began to publish what was expected of him. In a novel about the year 1863 he sneaked in a line that impressed a lot of people: that a nation has to mature not only to freedom but to slavery as well. I regard this sentence as capitulation. One ought not prepare himself for the role of slave. Anyway, Putinas wrote poems "for the drawer," which are now appearing in émigré journals. He translated Mickiewicz, served in the Academy of Sciences, and was catastrophically unhappy; he died after many years of this sort of life. He received an official funeral.

Another poet, Sruoga, ended up in a Nazi concentration camp from which he returned to Vilnius. He wrote a book about his experiences, which was quite interesting, cynical, and somewhat similar in tone to Borowski.[11] At a gathering for writers, a party official literally said that the Germans were right to put "such worthless people" into concentration camps. Sruoga died soon after this meeting.

There were a few brave ones, or the kind who felt they had nothing to lose, such as the old Russian émigré and religious philosopher Karsavin. These people, of course, perished. But others died too. In the end people grew accustomed to it all—to mandatory parades, forced friendships, to a special language diametrically opposed to what one really thought. There followed a period of accommodation and relative calm. People—in particular the educated class—accepted the constant lying as the coin that had to be paid to Caesar in exchange for a tolerable life. This behavior caused them no moral dilemmas, and perhaps this is what the authorities had in mind.

This was all a phenomenon of the newer, post-Stalinist era. But we must remember that in Lithuania Stalinism never really ended; it softened significantly in the 1960s, but since then stayed the same. I think the situation in Poland is quite different, and it's also a little different even in Russia. Within the Lithuanian intelligentsia, a feeling of helplessness and complete demoralization prevails. I cannot think of one member of the Lithuanian Academy of Sciences who would support Sakharov, even though there are some who marvel at him in their hearts. There is a convenient explanation for this: Sakharov is a Russian problem, and Lithuania is an occupied country with its own problems, so it is necessary to sacrifice everything in order to save the language and culture. Simply stated this means: keep quiet. Only it's not entirely clear whether a culture preserved in this way is worth anything.

The center of resistance in Lithuania lies elsewhere. Here I return to postwar Vilnius and my personal memories. I had often heard about the Partisan war in the Lithuanian forests. Actually, this should also have been a forbidden topic, but since it took on such enormous proportions, it was impossible to be completely silent about it. The authorities tried not only to suppress the Partisans but also to defame them in every possible way. It is still going on today: the surest way to success in official Lithuanian literature or film is to defame the Partisans, often perfidiously, because in doing so, they reveal parcels of the truth. This Partisan war was tragic and unbelievably savage. I heard of mass deportations (this was a strictly forbidden topic): I knew that people, mostly peasants, were shipped off to Siberia, where they have a hard life. One couldn't be oblivious to this. A few students from my class disappeared, and I found out that they had been deported with their families because the fathers had been officers in the former Lithuanian army. My father's brother was taken away to Siberia. Efforts were made to get him out, but they were unsuccessful. He died soon after, and his widow and daughter returned many years later. Friends who belonged to the old intelligentsia disappeared. Some returned, and a good number of them now write very loyal things.

You talk of the crime of 1940. We both know that the worst excesses of that crime occurred after the war. Every sixth Lithuanian was deported, they say. This was related to collectivization, but not only to that: above all, attempts were made to rid the nation once and for all of the habit of making decisions and of thinking of its own fate. This attempt was not very successful, and now it can be said that it was a failure, but certainly not because the authorities didn't try.

The Partisan effort was hopeless. The West, as we know, wasn't interested in the struggle of the Baltic countries. You wrote about this situation in *The Captive Mind*, for which every Lithuanian should be grateful. Unfortunately, no one listened as they should have. Even today I read woefully stupid disquisitions on the subject of the Baltic countries in the Western press. Westerners have grown accustomed to the thought that Russia always was and, in the name of holy peace, always should be on this territory, and that everything else is a meaningless episode. It's true that wiser voices are now being heard and probably more often than in the past. This is the redeeming influence of Solzhenitsyn and his kind. After the war, Lithuania bled more than the other Baltic countries. However, and perhaps *for* this reason, it has remained the most stubborn of them all. The war in the forest lasted until Stalin's death, actually even longer. The last Partisans held on literally until my day.

Little historical documentation remained after that war, and if it exists, then it is most likely buried in the depths of well-known archives. The fear of this kind of information is great. A few months ago in Vilnius the trial of a former Partisan took place. His name was Balys Gajauskas. He got a fifteen-year sentence for collecting archival material about the Partisan war. (It should be noted that he had already served a twenty-five-year jail sentence.) After the war, we heard that the area southwest of Vilnius near Druskininkai was in the hands of the Partisans. There were no Lithuanian Partisans around Vilnius or, in any case, far fewer than in other areas, because there the people did not consider themselves to be Lithuanians. Instead, a few regiments of the Polish Home Army were in the area, but their relationship with the Lithuanians was not always amicable. Yet the Lithuanian underground was operating in the city itself. I didn't really know anything about this underground, and it is only now that I am beginning to find out about it, but I felt that there was something in the air. A good friend of my father's, a poet named Kazys Boruta, wound up in jail because he knew things he would not reveal. This name is not foreign to you—as far as I know, you translated his poetry into Polish long ago. Even after a stint in Stalin's jails, Boruta remained a very honest man. At a meeting of Lithuanian writers where Pasternak was being attacked, he was the only one who got up and left. Boruta's friend, Ona Lukauskaitė, was tried with him and got ten years. She was released after Stalin's death. Not long ago and even though she was over seventy, she joined the Lithuanian Helsinki group.

The underground was, of course, infiltrated. A certain Markulis, who turned out to be a KGB agent, held the fate of many in his hands. Today he practices forensic medicine, that is, the preparation of cadavers. I know this sounds excessively literary, but, nevertheless, it is the truth. In the end everything was crushed. During my university days it was considered a matter of the past. People were sitting in the Gulag or lying in the graves; for those who survived, stabilization and accommodation began to take place, because the regime, using the words of Akhmatova, was changing over to a more vegetarian diet. Still, in 1959, at a gathering of the student assembly, it was announced that an organization was discovered in the philology department, which was engaging in enemy activities. The members of this organization were accused of discussing Lithuanian affairs and also apparently of writing manifestos. I didn't have any contact with these people—I hadn't even laid eyes on them—but I had already undergone a political transformation, so I felt some sympathy toward them. The embers of resistance smoldered for many years. This was not armed but ideological resistance. I regard this resistance as the only morally acceptable and effective kind. A nation cannot allow itself to be broken, spat upon, and ordered to give joyous thanks for this treatment. It is impossible to eradicate normal human reactions, especially the proverbial Lithuanian stubbornness and endurance—which has a seven-hundred-year history! Recently an extraordinary burgeoning of Lithuanian samizdat has taken place, which means that the resistance has acquired a new and important dimension. Now, it became more difficult not to notice the misfortunes of this country. I know that the Lithuanian intelligentsia, at any rate, the visible intelligentsia, cannot be credited for this new samizdat. There is also, in large numbers, the *homo sovieticus*, who modestly (or immodestly) grows rich, hosts foreigners with his heart on his sleeve, and in time, starts to travel abroad.

Silently and mortally he hates the Russians, but only Russians. The system is comfortable for him, because without it, he would not know what to do, at least for a time. But there are other people, for the most part simple, ordinary people.

I knew one of them, Viktoras Petkus. He had one of the most unusual personalities that I had ever encountered in my life. This large, phlegmatic Samogitian[12] spent fifteen years in the Gulag. He landed in jail the first time as an adolescent because of his connections with the underground, even though he carried no arms. After Stalin's death he was released, but soon after was arrested again, this time for having subversive literature in his home. This literature consisted of the works of Selma Lagerlöf as well as a book of Russian-Lithuanian poetry by Jurgis Baltrušaitis published in 1911. He sat it out for eight years. (In the meantime Baltrušaitis and Lagerlöf were rehabilitated.) Of course, after his release, he could not get a normal job, but he did put together one of the best private libraries of Lithuanian literature in Vilnius. He regarded his membership in the Lithuanian Helsinki group as the most natural thing, although he was convinced (as was everyone else) that he would be the first to go to jail for it. He was arrested. His trial took place at the same time as the trials of Ginzburg and Sharansky (who were, incidentally, his friends; he was also acquainted with Sakharov and was not a Russophobe). I was already in the West, in France. I could do nothing for him, except each morning as I read all the newspapers I could get a hold of, I felt the stature of Petkus grow. He did not answer the court's questions. He made it understood that in his opinion it was a court of the occupation and illegal, and he found it impossible to cooperate or associate with it. After that he either sat silent or slept. He got another fifteen years.

In Vilnius I often had the nagging feeling that the present inhabitants somehow did not belong to that city. They did not measure up to

Vilnius. I saw the world as deformed partly because of this, but, after all, this turned out to be untrue. We must remember that Vilnius is the center of Lithuanian resistance today, which I would categorize, without hesitating for a moment, as great. My own contacts with it were quite insignificant (although I conducted my own private war with this regime and played my own game of *va banque*). But resistance was in the air.

The authorities' relationship to Lithuanian nationalism was always duplicitous; with one hand the authorities tried to break its back, and with the other nourished it a little. Strange, temporary concessions were made, even during Stalinist times. I have already mentioned Gediminas Square. In 1940 "nationalism" was absolutely forbidden, yet during the war the authorities began to allow some nationalistic bombast (not only Russian, but also to a moderate extent, Lithuanian). Suddenly it became possible to praise great Lithuanian princes (after all, they had fought bravely against the Germans). All of this was very transparent (although one must add, also ambivalent). After the war, the situation became confused. Some of these concessions were simply tactical advances in the big game of subjugating the nation. At other times, it had to do with the maneuvering of the Lithuanian-Soviet elite, which quietly sabotaged Russification in its own interests. (As I mentioned, this elite is terribly anti-Russian, although all it takes is a little pressure to get them to do what's needed and even more.) Anyway, it is easier to govern by inciting the Lithuanians against the Poles, the Poles against the Lithuanians, and everybody against the Jews, and so on. (Concessions were also made to the Poles in the Vilnius area, although not great ones.) Russia is a great bugaboo: don't do this and that because the Russians will get you. Celebrations of folk song and dance flourish, of course, even in the form of highly aestheticized performances for the few, and the "Festival of Songs" is as important to the regime as the May Day parade. It became virtually forbidden to mention the great princes, but a castle was rebuilt in Trakai. This gesture infuriated Khrushchev, but his livid anger is only a memory. There was also a fad for historical drama with its various vague allusions, which nevertheless was approved of by the party censors and critics. In short, even in Lithuania nationalism is used as an added instrument of control (as well as safety valve), less so than in Poland, but still used . . . The relationship to Catholicism is much more explicit: you don't exploit Catholicism, you destroy it. And I think that both Catholicism and nationalism are the real forces in that part of the world.

I recall the tragicomic, deeply humiliating, and rather frequent vacillations of the so-called nationality policy, particularly when it came to symbols (the regime is extremely sensitive to symbols). The red flag on the Gediminas tower was replaced with a tricolored one, not the prewar Lithuanian flag, but a new one with a preponderance of red. After a while, emblems were returned to the cities, but that ended when it came to Vilnius's coat of arms, the St. Christopher. The national anthem, strictly forbidden after the first occupation, was played again after the war at parades in Vilnius, even in the worst of times. Later, it was replaced by a new one to which my father had written the words.

Here I must say a few words about my father. I cannot and will not judge him. I know that he had a very difficult life. In his youth he was a left-wing intellectual of the same cut as Kazys Boruta or Ona Lukauskaitė. A friend of his—a good one—was Pranas Ancevičius, before his escape to Poland. The world of the Kaunas-Wilno intelligentsia was really very small and interconnected. Hence, I had heard about Ancevičius from early childhood, though I had a rather distorted impression of him. In contrast to his friends, my father became an orthodox communist. I don't know what happened to him in 1940 when he took a seat in the Soviet parliament with Jędrychowski. It seems that the war had a decisive impact upon him, and after that he never changed. He recognized the existing situation as the only one possible. Still, he was not a cynic: he continued his friendship with Boruta, and Lithuania for him was not an empty sound. Moreover, his personal situation, and so mine as well, was somewhat precarious, because after Stalin's death he found out that a trial of the members of the old Left, which included him, was being prepared (it never came off). Those were difficult times. I must admit that I am more forgiving of the people of that generation than of today's upstarts—in any case, they had problems that today's people do not have.

The University of Vilnius. I began to attend the university, as I said, during an era of relative stability. Of course, my university years differed more from yours than yours did from Mickiewicz's. After 1939, the professors from the University of Kaunas (which was not a bad university) moved to Vilnius, but by my time they were no longer lecturing: they had emigrated, gone to Siberia, or simply no longer existed. A few, like the above-mentioned Putinas, were retired. Immediately after the war the standards—in the academic and every other sense—of the university dropped catastrophically. It is true that the lectures were given in Lithuanian, but they usually deteriorated into ideological chaff, or army drills. This began to change very slowly. There were a few professors of whom I cherish warm memories. One of these, Professor Balčikonis, a professor of Lithuanian and a lexicographer of the old school, was a weirdo, but a courageous person. As far as I know, he gave away most of his salary to the families of the repressed. He was one of those from Kaunas. Another was Professor Lebedys, an authority on the sixteenth and seventeenth centuries in Lithuania. I was examined in logic by Professor Sesemann, an old Russian émigré who had returned from Stalin's camps, where, they say, he managed to occupy himself with yoga and translating Aristotle (by heart) into Lithuanian. I am purposely writing only about the dead. After I had finished, the university established a school of Baltic studies, which attracted many students because it was considered patriotic and at the same time, so to speak, neutral (not all that neutral, however, for the head of the school, Professor Kazlauskas, drowned in the Wilia under mysterious circumstances).

The walls, beautiful library reading rooms, and the even more beautiful courtyards (nine or maybe even thirteen of them) preserved the aura of the old university. We used to say that there were places in that labyrinth where no human foot had ever stepped. The dormitory on Bouffal Hill, where I spent a lot of time, still stands. Not only did the architecture of the university survive, but also the library, which was mostly Polish (that changed somewhat later on). Many books ended up on the closed shelves, and therefore were virtually unobtainable. Even so, I found a lot of interesting things. I learned Polish very quickly, although most of my friends weren't interested in Polish. (It was easy for me because my maternal grandmother was Polish. She was an impassioned admirer of Sienkiewicz, and my father was able to read Polish and spoke a little.) Once I wrote a long paper entitled "Mickiewicz at the University of Wilno." Working on that paper, I read about a half of what could have been read on the subject, and in the process, I found out about the old Wilno Freemasons (the interwar Masons are for me terra incognita) and about the Scoundrels and Kontrym. After that, some friends and I established a club modeled after the Scoundrels, which was risky considering the ubiquitous eye of the KGB, but it somehow dissolved into schoolboy mischief and alcohol. At any rate, I knew of the traditions of that Wilno. However, at the same time, I had the feeling that my own tradition was nearer to Poška (Paszkiewicz),[13] a strange man, ridiculed by the Scoundrels, and

Daukantas (Dowkont),[14] who had connections with the Philomaths but went his own way, and who became the first Lithuanian historian. I was moved by the fate of this Daukantas, who was a rather comic figure touched with saintliness. Important to me was Donelaitis,[15] the eighteenth-century poet, who, in my opinion, was equal to the greatest in Europe. Here I must interject something about the language. Vilnius, which is now half-Lithuanian, speaks a strange koine, which is the result of the mingling in Vilnius of all the Lithuanian dialects and on which Slavic (and Soviet) jargon has, in turn, also had an effect. The new Lithuanian poetry is partly a rebellion against this koine (in which the poets are helped by the writers of earlier times) and partly a clever transformation of it. Nota bene, the Russian iamb does not bother me because the Lithuanian iamb also has a great tradition and is compatible with the spirit of the language. (Probably it is a matter of the accentual system, but I won't develop this any further because that would be linguistics.) Whatever way you look at it, Lithuanian literature, especially the literature associated with Vilnius, is my domain. Nevertheless, I left the university also with a love of Polish literature, and of Russian, too—and this was a great love.

Of course, no one taught me these things. Here I will recount my first political experiences. In school I joined the Komsomol, and it seemed to me that there was the way to achieve a better world. Virtually everybody had to join, and at the university they were a mixed group. These were not always the dullards and Stalinists, even though this element dominated and always had the last word. I belonged to the so-called true believers, who, I realize, were not numerous. The Twentieth Party Congress was for me and my friends a great shock (in spite of what we already knew), but I can give you the exact date of my conversion. It was the fourth of November, 1956, when the Hungarian uprising was quashed. Next came the Pasternak affair. Four of us wrote him a letter of admiration. At the time I had read all of his poems, and I had half of them memorized. We tried to produce a student literary almanac, which clashed with the censors and was publicly branded as "enemy." I was kicked out of the university for a year. This year was a godsend. I read day and night. During that time I discovered Russian poetry and, in general, what literature was all about.

Nadezhda Mandelstam likes[16] a game she devised: she asks everyone to name ten truly educated (and not old) people in the Soviet Union. As it turns out, there are only two: one a linguist and the other a specialist in Byzantine culture. Then Nadezhda gets to the point: both were ill throughout their childhood and did not attend Soviet schools. I didn't have that good fortune. But if I acquired any kind of education, I acquired it during that year. The university gave me only a basic knowledge of Lithuanian studies (incidentally, many of its areas remained inaccessible to me); I became acquainted with Marx, which I don't regret, and I studied classical philology. A friend and I even looked for a rabbi to give us some idea about Hebrew—but where was that rabbi to be found in postwar Vilnius? At any rate, it turned out that it was possible to learn something. You can swim against a Niagara of lies and useless information, and even swim out of it, but you can't drag anyone with you—everyone has to do it for himself. Here I admit that apart from Vilnius, Moscow was the other city that educated me. It is a very interesting city because, as Aleksandr Zinoviev[17] says, everything that the soul desires is there: Catholics and Buddhists, avant-gardists and dissidents, mathematicians and girls better than in Paris. True, most of those girls are now already in Paris, or in London. But jokes aside, Moscow was one hell of an experience.

I have one typical Soviet handicap—I'm not capable of speaking any foreign language (besides Polish and Russian), and now, in the

States, English comes to me with difficulty. True, I can read a few languages, but it seems to me that I am condemned to passivity, which torments me. Anyway, what good are these languages to a Soviet? Western books for him are available in ridiculously small quantities only, periodicals are totally unavailable, and as for travel—forget it! For that reason Polish turned out to be the most important language, and not for me alone. I knew quite a few people for whom Polish was the window to the world. Throughout the years, we met each other in the Polish bookstore on the Gediminka, and we also found books that were not available in this bookstore—like yours, for example. We discussed or joked with each other in Polish, partly to confuse undesirables, partly out of snobbery, and partly out of love for the Polish language because we were grateful to it.

Now I am coming to the problem of Polish-Lithuanian relations. For me personally, the antagonisms between our nations seem colossally stupid, and I would like to regard them as anachronistic. I think that a significant part of the younger generation in Lithuania does not feel any hostility toward the Poles. I suspect that it is the same the other way around; perhaps somewhere the feeling of Polish superiority and haughtiness still lingers, but perhaps not. We have passed out of that era and the old squabbles seem meaningless. Still, the problem is more complicated.

Lithuania attained national consciousness late, with great difficulty and in opposition to Poland. The influence of Polish culture, especially after the Union of Lublin (1569), was enormous. I think that in general it was positive, although no Lithuanian would agree with me on this point. Without Poland we would not have been aware of many things, and in all likelihood we would have had no idea of political laws. Our national rebirth had typically Polish overtones, at times Sarmatian and at times messianic, and paradoxically these models turned us against Polish cultural superiority. Everything had to be reversed: King Jagiełło, a hero for the Poles, was a traitor for us; a traitor, Janusz Radziwiłł, became a hero; and so forth . . . The nation had to learn to stand on its own feet, which it did clumsily at times, lapsing into childish complexes, which are easy to forgive because this happens to all nations in the beginning. Complexes, however, are long-lived and become ballast. You spoke of the memory of the Poles: well, the memory of the Lithuanians is even greater, and it goes back hundreds of years. We are proud of this, although it is not clear whether it is worth it. We remember that Polish cultural (as well as social) domination in Lithuania in the eighteenth century began to threaten the Lithuanians with the loss of their language and their historical direction. Add to that hundreds of years of painful national subordination, and what you get is a mania for greatness combined with a persecution complex. It is easy to laugh at this, although healthy ambitions can develop from it as well. Personally I do not have any feelings of national inferiority; the young Lithuanian generation is freeing itself from this, because now Lithuania is no worse than any other East European country. But certain stereotypes remain and can be revived, especially because the experience of totalitarianism in general does not foster wise and tolerant attitudes. There is a tradition of demonizing the Poles. According to this mentality (which still has influence, albeit vestigial), Poles throughout the centuries have had one goal: to annex Lithuania to Poland, denationalize it, and oppress it. The Poles are thought to be more dangerous than the Russians because they are Catholics as well as Europeans. The stereotype of the Machiavellian Pole, who always gets his own way if not by force then by treachery, lingers on. Here, in emigration, I often come into contact with this mentality, and I always feel a terrible shame because it is an immaturity straight out of Gombrowicz. A mature nation, which Lithuania undoubtedly is now, cannot be denationalized even if someone wanted it. This stereotype is one of inertia and regression, and can only be convenient to the regime. So, we and the Poles must remember about it, and we must avoid activities that incite and rekindle these feelings.

This problem, of course, is connected with Vilnius. There is a specific Lithuanian mythology about Vilnius, and I think that it plays a greater role in the history of that city than, for example, economic factors. For the Poles, Wilno was a cultural center on the eastern border of the country, important but nonetheless provincial. For the Lithuanians it is a symbol of continuity as well as historical identity— somewhat like Jerusalem. In the nineteenth and twentieth centuries, the Lithuanian imagination, to a considerable degree, was inspired by the myth of a royal and holy Vilnius, violently torn out of their hands. This myth doesn't always convince me, especially its monarchist part, but we have to agree that there is something in it. For example, Vilnius differs from Riga or Tallinn because it was not a Hanseatic center but a capital city, sacrosanct and the home of a great university. It was not a colonial center, and it grew naturally out of its terrain. So the debate about Vilnius includes the question, as you have already noted with regard to the city's historical position, whether it must be regarded only as a regional center or whether it should be included in the ranks of traditional East European capitals. And this question concerns the position and permanence of Lithuania. Lithuania without Vilnius is an ephemeral nation, but with Vilnius its past and its historical responsibility are secured.

There were no big battles between Poland and Lithuania, yet the problem of Vilnius was a serious one. The city gradually became a Polish (and also Jewish) enclave on Lithuanian soil. In the previously mentioned book, *Everything about Wilno in 1913*, only two Lithuanian names are mentioned: true, they were not just anybody, but Smetona and Basamavičius, the first signer of the Lithuanian Declaration of Independence. The language of the surrounding area in the nineteenth century was predominantly Lithuanian (while working on the Mickiewicz piece, I discovered this). The unraveling of this historical, ethnic, and social knot would have needed Solomonic heads which events had begrudged us, and besides, there wasn't enough time. Therefore, the course taken was unwise. The Lithuanians could not then, and cannot to this day, forgive either the Żeligowski episode[18] or the Polonizing zeal of Bociański and others. Moreover, they also could not understand Piłsudski's federalist ideal. They were right, since this was not the way to develop a federation, even if it had been possible, which I doubt. Conversely, they did not want to understand that the Poles had a right to Vilnius or Wilno, too, since Polish people and their culture predominated there. Forced Lithuanianization, like Polonization, would have been an unforgivable sin. At any rate, the stereotype of the "perfidious Pole" unfortunately became widespread at that time. The independent Lithuania considered itself to be like the Piedmont, whose purpose was to conquer Rome—alias Vilnius. This was not solely a matter of state; rather, it belonged to the realm of mass sentiment. And finally, Lithuanian determination by the irony of history triumphed under the most tragic circumstances.

Nowadays, however, it seems that both of us consider this dispute to be resolved. Having survived the twentieth century, Vilnius became a new city. It's true that it is still provincial, and even more so because the whole Soviet Union is terribly provincial. It continues to be an enclave, except now it is a Lithuanian-Russian enclave in a predominantly Polish region. Yet I have the hope that it will become the capital of a democratic Lithuania. The Lithuanians, under very difficult circumstances, have created the preconditions for that.

It is somewhat premature to talk about a democratic Lithuania, but

I think that we should recognize it as a possibility and a mission. We must think about new Polish-Lithuanian relations in this context. We must concentrate on the present, not the distant future, because the immediate future is the same fight with the totalitarian system, except that it is executed in more serious forms, a foretaste of which we have seen in Poland. Vilnius, that eternal enclave, would be given a new chance. As a city of ethnic regions overlapping each other, it is a model for all of Eastern Europe. Coexistence and mutual enrichment must replace the old frictions, and actually the antitotalitarian movement can be a great help in this. Let's take the Jewish question. You are right, Vilnius will never be the same without its Jewish district, ruined in part by the Germans and in part by the Soviets. Nonetheless, the few Jews who have remained in Vilnius are a significant group. Their relations with the Lithuanians are difficult because part of the Lithuanians (like the Poles, Russians, and others) committed crimes during the war. There are a variety of reasons for this which I will not go into now. It must be also said that there were hundreds of Lithuanians who saved Jews, at times risking their own lives. But a crime is a crime, and there is no getting around that. Lately, the television movie *Holocaust* created a stir among the Lithuanian émigrés, when it talked about a Lithuanian SS legion liquidating the Warsaw Ghetto. Officially, there was no such legion; there were only individuals, but this occasion was seized upon to "save the honor of the nation," as if anything could be redeemed by concealing, distorting, and blaming the Germans or even the Jews themselves. Without doubt, this proves the existence of complexes and a guilty conscience. For me, as someone speaking from the other side, this is all incomprehensible. Surely we have overcome this complex by now. We know several axioms. First, one cannot be silent about any crime. Second, there were and are collaborators in fewer and greater numbers, depending on the historical circumstances, but there is no such thing as a collaborating nation. Third, anti-Semitism and Sovietization come down to the same thing. The eradication of all traces of Jewish Vilnius, including what could have been saved, is an enormous loss for Lithuanian culture. And it is an absolute disgrace that the slaughter of the Jews is not mentioned officially; only the "innocent Soviet citizens" are remembered. Understanding these simple matters helps very much to solve the Lithuanian-Jewish problems and furthers day-to-day cooperation. Anti-Semitism in Lithuania, aside from the official line, is very weak today, and perhaps even dying out. Of course, a Jew would see this more clearly, but I have also heard this from Jews.

This same model can serve to improve the Polish-Lithuanian relationship as well as the Russian-Lithuanian relationship, even though the differences in each case are appreciable. The matter of Lithuanian-ness or Polishness is historically badly confused because the notion of "a Lithuanian" as well as the notion of "a Pole" changed over the centuries. In one sense Mickiewicz and Syrokomla[10] are Lithuanians; in another so are Witkacy, Gombrowicz, and Miłosz; in a third Pasz-kiewicz and Dowkont; and in a fourth we have today's Lithuanian writers. Oscar Miłosz is in a category of his own. One thing is clear: our nations are bound together and are unable to get along without each other. Having become a nation and a modern state, Lithuania had to emphasize that it differs from Poland. Today, however, this does not have to be emphasized because it is obvious. We must not scold one another because, as I said, this plays into the hand of the regime. You say that the new Lithuanian nationalism was by force of circumstance spasmodic and narrow-minded; perhaps it was not always so, because there were some attempts to have a dialogue with the Poles, to which their response was "never!" There were various unexpected rapprochements, among them personal and familial; but I agree that there was a good deal of fanaticism and stupidity, which is a part of every nationalism—French, Flemish, maybe Romansh, who knows? It is easier to forgive small countries but, one way or another, we should not excuse ourselves. Even so, we can say that "Central Lithuania"[20] is *plusquamperfectum*. We should also relegate the federalist dreams of the Regionalists to the past, because there are no more Regionalists in Lithuania today. The very fact of their existence was new to me, which may reflect badly on me, but everyone should agree that their program contained some valuable ideas that are worth remembering. A Finnish-Swedish solution would have been a good thing, but in all likelihood the chance was lost. The same thing is true for a Lithuanian literature in the Polish language (though it may be that such a literature does exist in a sense, and I would be inclined to include in this category your novel *The Issa Valley*). But above all, we should be realistic: the crux of this situation is the two hundred thousand Poles in the Vilnius area and twenty thousand Lithuanians in the Suwałki area. There are no aristocrats among them, virtually no intelligentsia: these are farmers and workers, people who have been trampled on by the regime but who deserve a decent life. I am outraged when I see the way the Lithuanians are treated in the Seinai region,[21] all the more so because it is the work of the Polish Church, which on other occasions has served the cause of freedom so well. But if at any time a forced and involuntary program of Lithuanianization begins in the Vilnius area (today there is none because it has been replaced by Russification), then I will be the first to say "no," and I hope that I won't be the only one.

You're right, it is easy to detect nationalism behind the official facade of prevarication in Eastern Europe. It is an ambivalent force, and a dangerous one. The whole value of world culture is in its variety of traditions and languages, but when language and ancestry become a fetish for salvation at the moment of slaughter, then I prefer to be one of the slaughtered. The humanization of national sentiment is a matter of utmost importance, and we must apply ourselves with great energy to this goal. Positive signs have appeared in the Lithuanian samizdat, which I have already mentioned, but at times one can hear the traditional voices, similar to the Endeks, but in reverse. By comparison, however, this happens less frequently than it does in the émigré groups, which is a consolation. The Lithuanian samizdat, while not the concern of the intelligentsia, nonetheless does come to intelligent conclusions. As for me personally, for some ten years in Lithuania I was, and in emigration still am, of course, accused of something like betrayal of my nation. The reason is that I'm a cosmopolitan, Judeophile, Polonophile—a Russophile even—and Lithuanians often irritate me simply because they are my people. The Lithuanian Helsinki group, to which I belonged, has been blamed because we were "not Lithuanian dissidents but all-Soviet dissidents." And how can it be any other way? The effort is hopeless unless it is joint, and we feel emotionally tied to everything that happens there. When I say there, I don't mean in the Soviet Union only, but in the whole of Eastern Europe. We are East European dissidents or simply East Europeans—which means the same thing.

Vilnius is one of the centers where a new East European formation is being created. Perhaps it was historically predestined for this. At any rate, you belong to this formation: you wrote about it more than once, and better than anyone else.

1978

Translated from the Polish by M. Ostafin (translation edited by T. Venclova)

NOTES—DIALOGUE ABOUT A CITY

1. Rootedness.

2. The Philomaths were a secret literary youth organization that existed in Wilno from 1817 to 1823. One of its members was the poet Adam Mickiewicz.

3. The Endeks were members of the National Democratic Party of Poland (Endecja), whose leader was Roman Dmowski.

4. The naturally "nationalistic" soul.

5. "Comrade" in Lithuanian.

6. "Sarmatian" is associated with the way of life, customs, and ideology of the Polish nobility of the seventeenth and eighteenth centuries, and connotes conservatism, backwardness, and traditionalism.

7. Gediminas was a Lithuanian prince of the fourteenth century, founder of Vilnius.

8. Three Crosses is a sculpture on a hill in Vilnius.

9. Laurynas Stuoka Gucewicz (1753–98), architect and principal representative of Lithuanian classicism, worked primarily in Vilnius. His major achievement was the building of the Vilnius Cathedral.

10. A Catholic holy site.

11. Tadeusz Borowski, the Polish author of books about Auschwitz.

12. A native of West Lithuania.

13. Dionizas Poška (Paszkiewicz) (1757–1830), a writer and active participant in the Samogitian national movement. His major work, "The Samogitian and Lithuanian Peasant," describes the oppression of the Lithuanian serf.

14. Simonas Daukantas (1783–1864), a historian, prose writer, and pioneer of the Lithuanian national revival. He was the author of the first history written in Lithuanian.

15. Kristijonas Donelaitis (1714–80), a classical Lithuanian poet and the first Lithuanian writer to be recognized in histories of European literature.

16. Nadezhda Mandelstam was still alive when this essay was written.

17. Aleksandr Zinoviev, a contemporary Russian dissident writer.

18. The Żeligowski episode was the name given to the military takeover of Lithuanian territory by General Lucjan Żeligowski (1865–1947). Despite the Suwałki Agreement, which called for an end to the armed struggle between Poland and Lithuania, Żeligowski, acting on a secret command from Piłsudski, entered Wilno on 9 October 1920 and created "Central Lithuania," which was subsequently joined to Poland.

19. Syrokomla (Ludwik Kondratowicz, 1823–62) was a minor Polish poet.

20. Central Lithuania was a semi-state entity (1920–22).

21. Seinai (Sejny) is a town in eastern Poland five kilometers from the Lithuanian border. The area around it is inhabited by Lithuanian speakers.

INDEX OF FIRST LINES

I suppose this never happened. Through the branches 34
It's roughly six o'clock, and the ice-covered road 37
I was welcomed by twilight and cold 23
Like the support of immortal souls 16
Midcentury has overtaken me 30
o the pillows and the palettes and the earrings made of gold 14
Outside the doorway ends the land 39
A projector flickers in the somewhat cramped hall 94
The shoots of grass pierce through the face and hands 13
Summer submerges the city 81
To the squares on our walls and floors 19
The twenty-four hours cross the middle, silence grows louder 5
We'll certainly return here. This is peace 52
We'll need them for quite some time yet: to make the path like a deck 9
We saw each other through another's words 17
We've been seized by the pull of the universe since September began 29
When even strangers lose the marks of strangeness 55
When, in private, tottering wisdom is sent from a height 45
When, in the midst of August, past 53
Winter over Europe. The expanse of asphalted fields 75
You wait for those who retreated? To the depths 3